Contents

Dedication. . . . .

Introduction 1

1. Engineering Design: Force, Motion, and Movement. 13

2. Engineering Design: Sound, Light, and Shadow 38

3. Engineering Design: The Built Environment
   and Construction 59

4. Technology: Knowledge and Innovation 76

5. Technology: Communication and Collaboration 88

Index 105

Dedication

To my favorite makers and tinkerers, Griffin and Cullen. Thank you for the inspiration!

CREATIVE INVESTIGATIONS
IN EARLY ENGINEERING AND TECHNOLOGY

Angela Eckhoff, PhD

Gryphon House
www.gryphonhouse.com

Published by Gryphon House, Inc.
P. O. Box 10, Lewisville, NC 27023
800.638.0928; fax 877.638.7576
www.gryphonhouse.com

Bulk Purchase

Gryphon House books are available for special premiums and sales promotions as well as for fund-raising use. Special editions or book excerpts also can be created to specifications. For details, call 800.638.0928.

Disclaimer

Gryphon House, Inc., cannot be held responsible for damage, mishap, or injury incurred during the use of or because of activities in this book. Appropriate and reasonable caution and adult supervision of children involved in activities and corresponding to the age and capability of each child involved are recommended at all times. Do not leave children unattended at any time. Observe safety and caution at all times.

Library of Congress Cataloging-in-Publication Data
The Cataloging-in-Publication Data is registered with the Library of Congress for ISBN 978-0-87659-755-2.

Introduction

The excitement level is high in Mr. Adams's classroom because the children are anxious to modify—by painting, cutting, and gluing—the found objects they have been collecting during the week. Mr. Adams and his students are working on a long-term project on recycling and reuse. For this part of the project, the children are using discarded objects to create three-dimensional (3-D) sculptures. They have been studying artists who create assemblage art out of natural and man-made materials—assemblage is art that is made by putting together dissimilar elements, often everyday objects, found and reinvented by the artist. As a design-based learning project, the assemblage project is an iterative process where the children are actively involved in every step: investigating the context through studying the need for recycling and reuse; learning about the ways in which people, including assemblage artists, reuse discarded objects; deciding what objects can be reused in art; collecting and sharing their found objects; thinking through and drafting designs for their artworks; modifying and assembling objects to create their artworks and reworking any aspect of their designs once they have assembled their artwork.

This marks the beginning of the point in the project where the children must transfer their 2-D drawings of their imagined artwork into a 3-D work using the objects they have collected and modified. The design-based nature of this project encourages the children to try out their ideas and revise or change them as necessary when they run into unexpected challenges. As a first step, Finn has decided to use brass door hinges to create a "robot family." In his drawing, he has the door hinges making up the torso of the robots. The robots are each different colors, so Finn decides that he must paint the hinges before assembling the robot. Finn carefully chooses colors that match the colors he drew on his robot sketch. As he paints, Mr. Adams checks in and asks Finn how the painting process is going. Finn shares that he is frustrated that the paint isn't drying quickly, so he won't be able to glue his pieces together today. Mr.

Adams pauses to remind Finn that the assemblage artworks don't have to be finished quickly and that he should take the time he needs to paint and put together his robot. "All week?" asks Finn, and Mr. Adams replies, "You can work on it all week and even into next week. Remember the artwork we looked at on the iPad? Those artists worked for months and even years designing and making those sculptures. You have to remember that your robot isn't going to lay flat, so you can see it from all sides." Finn stops painting and picks up one of his hinges; flipping it over, he says, "I'm going to paint the back too. It's the back of his robot shirt." "Right," says Mr. Adams. "Now you've got it; think it through!"

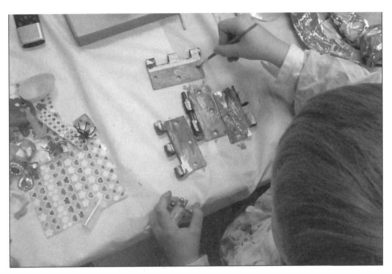

Finn reinvents the door hinges into colorful robot bodies.

As Mr. Adams shared with Finn, design-based learning is typically project based and encourages the students to work on a project over an extended period of time. Project-based work takes time. Ample time is needed so that students are provided the space to think deeply about a topic, problem, or area of interest. Often, in preschool classrooms, we don't provide children with enough opportunities to engage with their thinking at a deep level, but that can be changed when we integrate design-based thinking and project work into our daily routines. Design-based work connects well with content areas of engineering and technology as children engage in cycles of exploration, problem solving, and solution finding.

This book is designed to provide you with knowledge and lesson ideas that scaffold young children's experiences with engineering and technology while also building inquiry and creative thinking skills. You will find information on contemporary creativity and design-based pedagogical practices that early childhood educators can use to implement engineering and technology learning experiences for preschoolers. This book will broaden understandings of the relationship between engineering and technology content, the role of the learning environment, and supportive pedagogical practices for preschool-aged children. Many early childhood teachers are uncertain about whether engineering and technology experiences are developmentally appropriate for preschoolers and when and how they should introduce these topics to their students. When engineering and technology experiences build upon student interests and connect to other areas of content learning—literacy, science, the arts, mathematics, and social studies—young children are able to experience meaningful connections among each content area.

This book stresses the importance of encouraging minds-on learning experiences in the early childhood classroom through guided and independent investigations where every child is actively involved in meaningful ways. Early childhood educators have important roles in early engineering and technology experiences and will act as both guides and facilitators throughout the planning, implementation, and assessment of the creative, design-based experiences presented throughout this book. For young children, technology experiences involve using tools, identifying and acting on problems, being creative and inventive, and making things work. Engineering experiences involve exploring problems, using a variety of materials, and designing and building things that work.

Creative Investigations in Early Engineering and Technology will support your development of creative engineering and technology experiences in the classroom by helping you to:

- understand the links among engineering content, design learning, and project-based learning.

- plan cooperative engineering and technology lessons that will engage all children in your classroom as individuals or when working in small or whole groups.

- implement classroom experiences that support children's engagement with engineering and technology in everyday experiences.

- recognize children's understandings of engineering and technology concepts to build upon their current understandings to support knowledge growth.

- document children's knowledge development with authentic work samples and classroom artifacts.

Playful Learning

Play is an important element for learning in early childhood. Through play, young children learn about themselves, their environment, people, and the world around them. Playful learning encourages children to explore and experiment in situations where they feel comfortable taking risks and delving into the unknown. Children's play in the early childhood classroom can take on many different forms and functions. When children explore, experiment, and cooperate through play, they learn about how the world works. Children need teachers who are supportive of children's play and who work to carefully identify play situations where teacher guidance or involvement are welcome and needed.

Young children use their knowledge and understandings by bringing these ideas into their play to further experiment and clarify their understandings. This process is child driven; the role of the adult is one of supporter, guide, and facilitator. The adult meets each child at his own stage of understanding with intentional pedagogical practices that promote questioning and exploration. Teachers can create early childhood classrooms that honor the ways in which children learn and explore by ensuring that young children have ample opportunities for playful learning and exploration. In the role of supporter, guide, and facilitator, the teacher

Creative Investigations in Early Engineering and Technology

carefully observes children's play and helps to scaffold children's thinking through questioning and by providing opportunities for guided learning with additional supportive materials.

Design Learning

You may have heard of the terms *problem-based learning, discovery learning, project-based learning,* and *design-based learning.* These are all approaches to curriculum and lesson development that come from a constructivist learning model where students are actively involved in the process of discovery. In early childhood settings, the ideas of design-based approaches can be directly linked to our use of project-based learning. In design-based approaches in early childhood classrooms, young children learn what they need to learn in a "just-in-time" manner while taking the next steps in the learning process. Essentially, design-based experiences are authentic and hands on; have clearly defined outcomes that allow for multiple solution pathways; promote student-centered, collaborative, thinking-focused work; include familiar and easy-to-work-with materials; allow for multiple design iterations to improve the work; and have clear connections to science, technology, engineering, and math concepts, or STEM. For young learners, design challenges can involve problem-solving tasks that are complex, open ended, and have no one correct pathway to a solution. Teachers play a critical role in design learning and project-based work because the teacher needs to be supportive and encouraging throughout the cycle of problem exploration and solution finding. In this supportive role, teachers can work to provide children with needed materials, provide time and space for exploration, and scaffold student thinking through close observation and open-ended questioning.

Building Creative Engineering and Technology Experiences in the Classroom

Early childhood educators have essential roles in the development of children's creative thinking skills because they can create supportive classroom environments or classrooms in which children's creative skills are not stifled. To incorporate creative learning experiences in the classroom, teachers must design lessons that include opportunities for critical thinking and reflection while also maintaining a focus on student interest. In addition, teachers must recognize that creativity is a learning process that encourages social interaction and promotes individual ownership of ideas. In the classroom, creativity is a part of the learning process based upon children's interests and involves reflection and interaction with other children and adults and requires children to document and report on their thinking and experiences. When young children are provided opportunities to personally engage with challenging, reflective learning experiences, they are building critical and creative thinking skills.

The lesson ideas and classroom vignettes shared throughout this book incorporate opportunities to build children's understandings of shape, structure, location, motion, and transformation and also promote children's inquiry and creative thinking skills. Each lesson includes critical elements of inquiry and creative thinking—open-ended tasks and opportunities for social interaction, reflection, and elaboration. Open-ended tasks provide young learners with opportunities to experiment with new ideas and engage in inquiry. Because open-ended tasks promote idea experimentation, they encourage children to focus on the processes of learning rather than the need to arrive at a solitary correct answer. Gaining experience with idea experimentation will help support children's acceptance of ambiguity and willingness to make mistakes, allowing them to gain confidence in their problem-solving abilities. Likewise, providing opportunities for small-group works and social interaction is a crucial component of creative thinking. Working in pairs or small groups will help to promote brainstorming and allow children to learn from and with each other. Such tasks will also support children's experiences with reflection and idea elaboration. These skills are important cognitive tools that allow children to learn from their own experiences and examine their own learning processes. Employing these components of creativity in the classroom will help to create a rich, engaging learning environment for all students.

Recommended Practices and Content Coverage in Early Engineering and Technology

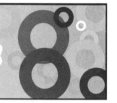

The content of the lessons presented in each chapter of this book is based upon recommended practices by the National Association for the Education of Young Children (NAEYC, 2012), the International Society for Technology in Education standards for students (ISTE, 2016), and the *Next Generation Science Standards* (NEXTGen) from the National Academies Press (2013). While many of the standards recommended by these organizations don't speak directly to young children in the preschool years, we can use these guidelines to help determine the types of experiences that we can develop and encourage in our classrooms so that our students have a solid foundation in both content understandings as well as experiences engaging in critical and creative thinking processes. Every lesson presented throughout each chapter is designed to encourage you to explore and implement the types of open-ended engineering and technology experiences that will build children's thinking, exploration, questioning, and documentation skills in addition to curricular content knowledge. Together, we will explore the types of lessons and approaches to pedagogy that will help your students learn much more than the conceptual facts; we will look for the opportunities that arise during your interactions with students where you can support, extend, and encourage their thinking with conversation and questioning in a natural manner.

Every lesson you encounter in this book will ask you to carefully consider your interactions with young children as well as the classroom environment. The interplay among children, teachers, and the classroom environment are all central to the process of learning. The concept of *possibility thinking* encourages teachers to consider how asking questions, play, supportive classrooms, imagination, innovation, and risk taking have on the processes of thinking and learning.

- **Possibility thinking**—a dynamic interplay between children and teachers (Craft, et al., 2012)

- **Posing questions**—questions from children are acknowledged and celebrated by teachers. Teachers' questions encourage inquiry.

- **Play**—opportunities for extended play periods

- **Immersion**—immersion in a benign environment free from criticism and mockery

- **Innovation**—teachers closely observe evidence of new ideas in student thinking to prompt and encourage

- **Being imaginative**—ample opportunities to meld creative new ideas and curriculum content

- **Self-determination and risk taking**—deep involvement and risk taking are encouraged by both children and teachers

Source: Craft, Anna, Linda McConnon, and Alice Matthews. 2012. "Child-Initiated Play and Professional Creativity: Enabling Four-Year-Olds' Possibility Thinking." *Thinking Skills and Creativity* 7(1): 48–61.

Promoting Creative, Design-Based Learning with Technology and Engineering

Classroom Components	Supportive Approaches in the Early Childhood Classroom
Physical Environment	• Flexible spaces with moveable furnishings that provide room for exploration, display, and storage, and spaces that can accommodate and adapt for small and large groups

Classroom Components	Supportive Approaches in the Early Childhood Classroom
Role of the Teacher	<ul><li>Provide opportunities for children to document their thinking through drawing, writing, and verbal means</li><li>Encourage students to share their thoughts with a large/small group</li><li>Provide materials that can support student inquiry</li><li>Closely monitor student thinking and exploration to scaffold experiences</li></ul>
Peer-to-Peer Relationships	<ul><li>Provide opportunities for children to share their problem-solving experiences and encourage and support children's use of design-based and creative thinking</li><li>Provide opportunities for children to ask questions, work out trials/planning, work in pairs/small groups, and plan experiments</li></ul>
Structure of Technology and Engineering Experiences	<ul><li>Provide opportunities for children to connect technology and engineering to other content areas, work on problems and projects for extended periods of time, and revisit previous experiences and lessons multiple times to encourage mastery and promote confidence</li></ul>
Parent and Community Engagement	<ul><li>Provide opportunities to connect technology and engineering experiences with the community and the children's daily lives</li><li>Engage the family throughout the learning process through regular documentation of children's experiences</li></ul>

Creating Engaging Engineering and Technology Learning Centers

In addition to planning and implementing targeted engineering and technology lessons in the classroom, it is important to create learning spaces where your students are able to further their own explorations. Learning centers are a good place to invite your students to work individually or in small groups; these centers can be permanent or moveable, depending on the interests and needs of your students at any given time. While many preschool classrooms have math, science, literacy, dramatic play, and art centers, the disciplines of engineering and technology are a less frequent inclusion. However, you can create stand-alone engineering and technology centers or integrate them into the learning spaces you already have in the classroom. The best way to determine which type of center most fits your current needs is to evaluate the actions and interactions of your students. For example, if you've introduced a new app or program that the children expressed interest in, you can capitalize on their excitement and create a space where several children can work together with the digital media. Or, perhaps you want to introduce an iPad or tablet into the writing center in the hopes of attracting students to the center who might not otherwise join.

Engineering concepts find a natural extension to preschoolers' play in the block area or in outdoor spaces where children have access to large blocks or moveable equipment. In addition, digital cameras and audio recorders can fit into every learning space in your classroom, providing a unique benefit based on location. For example, digital cameras in your outdoor play space can prompt students to think about and examine earth and life-science concepts. Those same cameras placed in your art or dramatic play center can serve to document children's creative processes.

Consider the following elements in the implementation and integration of engineering and technology into your classroom's learning spaces:

- **Workspace**—Depending upon your classroom size and setup, engineering and technology learning spaces may be permanent or spaces that need to be set up and broken down each day—especially if you are using tablets, iPads, or digital cameras and don't want to leave that equipment out. It is important to ensure that children have enough space to use materials and media without becoming frustrated, if you'd like to invite pairs or small groups to work together. You'll also want to ensure that you have tabletop spaces for any technology equipment and plenty of floor space for materials used in building and construction.

- **Consider the walls**—When children engage in design and project-based work, it is important to share documentation of the processes of learning and exploration to remind them of where they began and to encourage them to continue their work. Classroom walls are an excellent place to display photographs, drawings, and examples from children's work generated during classroom engineering and technology experiences. When displayed, children can be encouraged to use these materials to support and extend their explorations. Classroom displays can also help to connect and inform families to the work of the children.

- **Books and print materials**—Children's books featuring engineering and technology content should be accessible to children. Additionally, children's journals can be placed in the classroom so that children have easy access to their own work. Students should each have a journal dedicated to STEM explorations.

Intentionally designed engineering and technology spaces for learning will provide children opportunities to extend and continually explore the concepts introduced during planned lessons at their own pace and interest level. Revisiting ideas and concepts during play is very important to the process of knowledge building. Young children need opportunities to explore ideas, ask questions, and experiment in playful settings.

Engineering and technology learning spaces can support children's opportunities to:

- Explore and learn, based on learner interests

- Engage in discovery and construction of meaning

- Extend activities from the lessons

- Explore concepts from the lessons or related concepts in depth

- Connect engineering and technology to daily experiences

Organization of the Book

The book is based upon broad categories for early engineering and technology explorations: force, motion, and movement; sound, light, and shadow; the built environment and construction; knowledge and innovation in technology; and communication and collaboration in technology.

Each chapter begins with a section where you can find background information on engineering and technology content. Each chapter also features classroom vignettes to help bring the information on content and pedagogical information to life. Woven throughout the book are engineering and technology lessons for preschoolers that are built upon pedagogical practices for inquiry, creativity, and design-based thinking. You will also find information on recommended children's books related to each chapter's content.

1
Engineering Design: Force, Motion, and Movement

Young children experience movement throughout their day as they run, jump, slide, crawl, and skip. These gross motor movements serve as a foundation to understanding how and why objects move in different ways. As a child pushes a friend on a swing or pulls open a door, she is applying a force to cause movement. *Motion* is the scientific word used to describe types of movement. Motion can only be applied if there is a push or pull force. There are two types of force—*contact forces* (forces that touch when applied) and *at-a-distance forces* (forces that don't touch when applied). In early childhood, young children can engage with design-based experiences that will help develop their foundational understandings of force and motion.

Experiences with engineering concepts provide creative opportunities for project-based learning by incorporating hands-on design and construction that can promote problem solving with two-dimensional and three-dimensional objects. Design-based engineering experiences can integrate other content areas such as math, science, and literacy to engage students in learning by applying concepts, skills, and strategies to explore real-world engineering and design concepts.

Understanding Motion and Force

Movement is a natural source of interest and exploration for young children, who spend their days in a whirlwind of gross and fine motor play. Motion is an important concept for young children to explore because it affects all of our lives daily. *Motion* is best defined as the change in a position or location of an object. However, objects do not change their locations of their own accord. Force is needed to effect the change in location, and there are numerous categories of force that can help us to understand how motion works.

Action-at-a-Distance Forces

There are three action-at-a-distance forces—gravity, magnetism, and electrical—and these forces do not require direct contact between the objects to enact motion.

- **Gravity:** Gravity is force that pulls two objects with mass toward each other and works the same on all objects unless some kind of resistance gets in the way. A gravitational force can pull objects that are far from each other, such as how the moon's gravity affects ocean tides, or can be felt closer but still at a distance, such as how the earth's gravity pulls a child toward the ground when she jumps off a swing.

- **Magnetism:** A magnetic force can either pull opposite ends of two magnets together or push the matching ends apart from a short distance away from each other. The magnetic field of a magnet can create a magnetic force (attraction) on other objects with magnetic fields, such as a paper clip. The paper clip becomes a temporary magnet for as long as it is touching the real magnet and can be used to attract more paper clips. If the paper clip is removed from the magnet, it will lose its magnetic force.

- **Electrical force:** An electrical force is an attractive or repulsive force between two charged objects. Similar to magnetism, electric forces are attractive when two objects have opposite charges and are repulsive when two objects have like charges. As an example, static electricity is easy to observe in the winter when children come in from outside and remove their knit hats. As they remove the hats, their hair will stand on end from the attractive force.

Contact Forces

There are six kinds of forces that act on objects when they come into direct contact with each other.

- **Normal force:** A normal force is the support force exerted upon an object that is in contact with another stable object. For example, a bookshelf exerts an upward force upon a book to support the weight of the book.

- **Tension force:** A tension force is the force that is transmitted through a rope or wire when it is pulled tight at opposite ends. The tension force is directed along the length of the wire and pulls equally on the objects on the opposite ends of the wire.

- **Applied force:** An applied force is force that is put to an object by a person or another object—a push or pull motion moves an object.

- **Frictional force:** A frictional force is the force exerted by a surface as an object moves across it or attempts to move across it. For example, if a ball slides across the surface of the floor, the floor exerts a friction force in the opposite direction that the ball is rolling, causing the ball to slow and eventually stop.

- **Spring force:** A spring force is the force created by a compressed or stretched spring upon any object that is attached to it. Depending upon how the spring is attached, it can pull or push to create a force. As an example, a spring in a retractable pen makes the pen tip extend and retract when pushed.

- **Air-resistance force:** An air-resistance force is a type of frictional force that acts upon objects as they travel through the air, such as leaves traveling along on a windy day in autumn.

Movement

The concepts of velocity and inertia are important to understanding the physical movement of objects. An object's *velocity* is how fast it is moving through space in a particular direction. When the object changes direction, such as when turning left or right, the velocity is changed because it is no longer moving in its original direction. Inertia is a property of all objects that is related to the object's own mass. The more mass something has, the more inertia it has and the harder it is to push or pull. *Inertia* is a measure of how difficult it is to change an object's velocity. An object with less mass will require less force to speed it up or down than an object with greater mass.

Engineering experiences with force and motion can take place throughout the day during both free play and planned experiences as children play and work together. Many of the materials you will need to involve your students in force and motion are already used in early childhood classrooms. As you plan activities involving force and motion, consider the guidance from the related *Next Generation Science Standards* from the National Academies Press. While these standards are written to guide K–12 learning experiences, the disciplinary core ideas that they are based upon can be a helpful guide for preschool engineering experiences as you work to help build children's foundational knowledge and creative thinking skills.

Core Ideas in Engineering

Forces and Motion

- Pushes and pulls can have different strengths and directions.

- Pushing or pulling on an object can change the speed or direction of its motion and can start or stop it.

Creative Investigations in Early Engineering and Technology

Types of Interactions

- When objects touch or collide, they push on one another and can change motion.

Relationship between Energy and Forces

- A bigger push or pull makes things speed up or slow down more quickly.

Defining and Delimiting Engineering Problems

- A situation that people want to change or create can be approached as a problem to be solved through engineering.

- Asking questions, making observations, and gathering information are helpful in thinking about problems.

- Before beginning to design a solution, it is important to clearly understand the problem.

Developing Possible Solutions

- Designs can be conveyed through sketches, drawings, or physical models. These representations are useful in communicating ideas for a problem's solutions to other people.

Optimizing the Design Solution

- Because there is always more than one possible solution to a problem, it is useful to compare and test designs.

Source: NGSS Lead States. 2013. *Next Generation Science Standards: For States, By States.* Washington, DC: The National Academies Press.

Vignette for Understanding: Straw Gliders and Movement

Lucas is working in the classroom's engineering center alongside his friend Max, designing and building paper and straw-paper gliders. Their teacher, Ms. Meghan, has placed a few design plans for different airplanes along with a variety of materials in the center. She invited the

children to use paper and pencils to sketch out their planes before beginning their construction. Sample design plans for both paper airplanes and the straw glider are hung on the wall over the children's workspace. Lucas's sketch plan of his straw glider lies on the table in front of him, while Max is carefully sketching his design for a paper airplane. Lucas gets started cutting two long strips of paper of equal lengths that he will use to create the loops he needs for either end of his glider. He uses tape to secure the ends of the paper loops together, while Max helps by holding the ends together. He tapes the loops on either end of his straw and announces that he is ready to fly his glider. Ms. Meghan walks Lucas out to the hallway, and Lucas pulls his arm back and forces the glider forward. It flies for a few seconds before floating to the ground, and Lucas cries out in disappointment, "No, no. Fly more!" As he walks to pick up his glider, Meghan asks if she can take a look at it quickly: "Okay, I see you made two big loops. Have you looked carefully at the design plan in the center?" As they walk back to the center together, Lucas insists that he did match his design to the design plan. Once in the center, they join Max in looking over the plans. Max notices that the plan for the straw glider has one small loop and one bigger loop, which is different than Lucas's design. Lucas asks why the size of the loops would matter, and Meghan directs the boys to think about the design of the other paper airplanes, asking "Do you notice any patterns with the front and back of these planes that you fold?" Max responds that the front of the plane is smaller than the back when you fold regular paper airplanes. Lucas agrees that he notices the same thing and states that he is going to make new gliders with loops of different sizes to see if having a smaller loop in the front and a bigger loop on the back will give his plane more power. Ms. Meghan encourages Lucas to think about how the bigger loop might help keep his plane level in the air just like the wings on the paper airplane Max is folding. Before leaving to help another child, Ms. Meghan encourages Lucas and Max to keep track of their plane designs and trials in their planning notebooks so that they can compare their flight results.

Lucas builds his straw plane.

Reflection

Lucas's understanding of aerodynamics and design are deepened after his plane doesn't fly as long as he had hoped, and he has to return to his original design sketch. With assistance from Max and Ms. Meghan, Lucas is able to understand why his built plane was not flying as expected. This analysis will help grow the boys' understanding of how important it is to follow a design exactly.

Motion and Design Across the Curriculum: Planning Tips

Interactions with force and motion can involve many different types of materials and simple machines (lever, wheel and axle, pulley, inclined plane, wedge, and screw) that can be made out of classroom materials. Creating a classroom STEM center or, specifically, an engineering and design center is a good pedagogical strategy for encouraging children to build and explore during independent investigations. Ample space will be a necessary consideration when planning your engineering and design center because children will need space to plan out and build with materials. Such a center can house blocks of various sizes, paper or plastic tubes; small toy cars; balls; building materials such as K'nex, Tinker Toys, and Lego bricks; boxes of various sizes; gears and wheels; straws and craft sticks; tape; rubber bands; sketch paper; and pens.

Questions for Inquiry and Exploration in Motion

The following are a brief listing of questions that can be used to encourage guided-inquiry explorations with motion:

- Do you think it will move fast or slow? Why do you think that?

- Will a light push move the ball the same distance as a big push?

- What can I do to find out which of these will help the ball roll the farthest?

- Will the car roll in a straight line or curved line? Why do you think that?

- What can you do to change the direction the ball is rolling?

Lesson Ideas

The Way I Move Game

Topic:

Motion can be observed, described, and measured

Objective:

Children will identify the different ways an object can move—a straight line, curved line, zigzag, up and down, back and forth, and fast and slow.

Materials:

3 different colors of masking tape

Overview:

This lesson works best if children play in pairs or small groups so that they don't spend too much time waiting and have multiple opportunities to walk a movement line.

Creativity Skills:

Exploration

Visualization

Activity Steps:

1. Prior to playing the game, use masking tape to mark off three lines—straight, curved, and zigzag—that are about five feet in length.

2. Invite the children to take turns walking each line, one at a time.

3. Encourage them to name their movements. If this is their first time playing, assist them in naming their movements.

4. You can also challenge them with suggested movements—Can you move back and forth on the zigzag line? Can you move fast on the curved line?

Documentation:

Take anecdotal notes about the children's ability to name or identify the various movements.

Extension Lesson:

This lesson can be extended by inviting the children to move along with music on the lines. This extension will work best if the lines are extended so that the children will have more space to enact their movements.

Making a Maze Tilt Game

Topic:

Motion and speed

Objective:

Children will create a small maze that will allow them to tilt a platform to move a ball through the game.

Materials:

Loose parts (bolts, nuts, screws, wooden craft sticks, twigs, pipe cleaners, cut straws of varying lengths)

Sketch paper (or STEM journals) and pencils

Tape or adhesive

Small plastic, Styrofoam, or paper tray

Small rubber balls

Creativity Skills:

Exploration

Visualization

Solution finding

Strategic planning

Collaboration

Documentation

Overview:

Children will work in pairs so that there is adequate access to needed materials and cooperation with a peer.

Activity Steps:

1. Begin by asking children if they've ever seen a pinball or a marble maze tilt game. If they have, invite them to talk about their experiences. If not, show them examples and talk about the objective of the game and the movements involved.

2. If they haven't played this type of game before, it can be helpful to create an example of the game so they can practice playing before planning their own design.

3. Encourage the children to sketch out an example of their game before attaching their chosen materials to the tray.

4. As they look through the loose parts, ask them to consider how they might use the object as part of their maze.

5. Invite them to consider how the balls might respond to a curved pipe cleaner or a straight craft stick—will it roll straight or move in a curved line? How far will they need to tilt their tray to have the ball move? Do they think the ball will move fast or slow if they tilt the tray just a little?

6. Periodically check in with the children during planning and building. Once they complete their built maze, encourage them to invite other children to play their game.

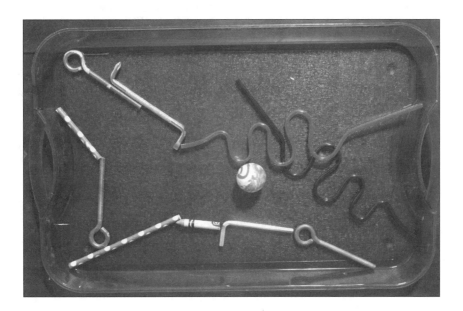

Documentation:

Take anecdotal notes about the children's ability to plan, problem solve, and collaborate during building.

The children's own built mazes can also serve as a source of documentation.

Extension Lesson:

This lesson can be extended by inviting the children to build a maze outdoors with ropes, playground cones, and other equipment that they can kick a ball through.

Reclaimed Materials Catapult

Topic:

Motion and force

Objective:

Children will use reclaimed materials to put together a catapult to change the direction or motion of small objects.

Materials:

Wooden craft sticks

Wooden paint stirrers

Rubber bands

Soda bottle lid

Glue or hot glue adhesive
Safety note: Hot-glue guns are for adult use only.

Pompoms, cotton balls, and other small materials for launching

Small basket

Creativity Skills:

Exploration

Visualization

Solution finding

Strategic planning

Collaboration

Documentation

Overview:

This lesson will work best in a whole-group setting because adult assistance will be needed to put together the catapult.

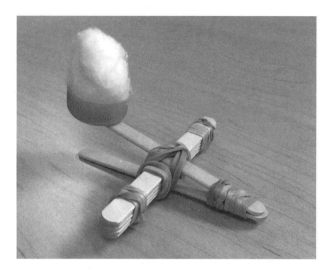

Activity Steps:

1. To ensure that each launch is safe, it is best to place a target on the ground—a small basket will work fine—for the children to aim at before launching. Be sure to emphasize that this is a game where children take turns, and every launch is to be aimed at the target only.

2. Ask the children if they've ever heard the word *catapult* or seen a catapult. Explain that a catapult helps move objects.

3. Use wooden craft sticks to make a small catapult, or use wooden paint stirrers to make a larger catapult.

4. Invite a child to count out five craft sticks and stack them on top of each other. Place a rubber band on each end and tighten until the stack holds together tightly.

5. Next, place one craft stick on top of another and wrap a rubber band around one end. Slide the larger stack of sticks through the open end of the two craft sticks.

6. Wrap a rubber band around the stack of craft sticks to the open, upper craft stick.

7. Glue the soda bottle lid to the top of the upper craft stick; the lid will serve as a basket to hold the small items to be launched.

8. Once it is dry, invite the children to come up in pairs to try out the catapult.

9. Ask one child to hold down the base of the catapult while another child loads and pulls back the top to launch the items.

10. Talk to the children about the force used to pull back the top of the catapult and how far their objects travel. Encourage children to make predictions on how far their launched objects will travel. Will the building block go farther than the cotton ball? Why do you think that? Let's try it out.

Documentation:

Take anecdotal notes about the children's ability to collaborate during building and launching as well as of their understandings of force and motion during their launches.

Extension Lesson:

Extend the lesson by placing the catapult in the STEM area, and invite the children to record their launches in their STEM journals. Provide standard or nonstandard measurement tools so they can record the distances their objects travel.

Balls and Ramps

Topic:

Motion and speed can be observed, described, and measured.

Objective:

Children will identify the different ways a small ball can move—along a straight line, curved line, zigzag, and fast and slow.

Materials:

Wooden or plastic planks

Wooden blocks of varying widths

Small balls—rubber, golf, ping-pong, tennis, marble

Standard measurement tools—tape measure or yardstick

Nonstandard measurement tools— string or rope

STEM journal and pencils

Masking tape

Overview:

This lesson can be completed in pairs, as individuals, or in a whole group. You will need a large space for the children to build and use the ramps.

Activity Steps:

1. Invite the children to create a simple ramp or inclined plane by placing a wooden block underneath one end of a plank.

2. Invite the children to talk about which ball will roll the farthest. Often, young children will make assumptions based upon their preferences. For example, a child might guess that the golf ball will roll the farthest because it is yellow, and yellow is his favorite color.

3. This is a great opportunity to set up a trial—testing a white golf ball and a yellow golf ball to see if the color of the ball has an influence on how it rolls. It is important to design trials that are based upon the children's beliefs and assumptions rather than to simply inform them that color, for example, is irrelevant to the manner in which a ball will roll down a ramp.

4. One at a time, the children will hold the ball at the top of the ramp and release it. When the ball comes to a stop, mark its resting position with a piece of masking tape, or invite the children to measure the distance rolled.

5. They can record the results of their trials in their STEM journals.

6. Be sure to invite the children to take time to draw images of the balls alongside the numbers they record so that they can easily recall the type of ball associated with the distance recorded.

7. Repeat trials using the different balls, and vary the slope of the incline by adding or removing supporting blocks.

Documentation:

Take anecdotal notes about the children's ability to name or identify the various movements and distances the balls traveled. The children's STEM journals can also be used as supportive documentation.

Extension Lesson:

This lesson can be extended by covering the ramps with differing textured materials—sandpaper, bubble wrap, wax paper, and aluminum foil—or by varying the surface the ball will roll onto—carpet, wood flooring, or linoleum.

Protect the Egg!

Topic:

Introduction to gravity, air resistance, and design challenges

Objective:

Children will design, build, and test a covering to protect a raw egg from a high fall. The children will make simple predictions and record the results of the test drops.

Materials:

Recycled materials (cardboard boxes, tubes, newspaper, cloth material)

Adhesive materials (glue, tape)

String, rubber bands

Raw eggs

Digital camera for stills or video

Sketch paper and pencils

Overview:

This lesson works best if children plan in small groups so that you have at least two trials in your classroom.

Activity Steps:

1. Talk with the children about what happens when an item drops, using examples from their own lives—jumping off playground equipment, dropping an object from a table, throwing a ball into the air.

2. This is a great time to introduce the word *gravity* and talk about its meaning—the gravity of the earth pulls objects toward the center of the planet.

3. Following your discussion, talk with the children about performing a fun experiment. You can begin by showing an egg and asking whether anyone has ever dropped an egg. If so, what happened to the egg?

4. Let them know that they are going to work together to build a protective container to stop the egg from breaking when it is dropped from a high height. You can even show images of other egg-drop containers found on the internet to help them begin the design process.

5. Working with the small groups, help the children explore the qualities of the available materials as they think about their design. Encourage the children to sketch their designs, as the group will need to agree on a final design before building. The design and building process will take place over several days, so encourage the children to take their time during each phase of the project.

6. Once a final design is developed and agreed upon, invite the children to use the recycled materials to build their containers.

7. On the day of the test trials, ask the children to present their designs to the rest of the class so that differences across designs can be compared.

8. To test, place a raw egg inside the built containers and drop from a standardized height (top of a stairwell or playground climbing equipment).

9. After the drop, check to see if the container protected the egg. Encourage the children to revise their designs and conduct additional test drops if needed.

Documentation:

The children's sketched designs and video or still pictures from the test drops can serve as documentation. Anecdotal notes from conversations with the children during the design and test phases can also serve as project documentation.

Extension Lesson:

This lesson can be extended by inviting families to take part in the design and experimentation process. You can send information home to parents about the design challenge of building a protective covering for an egg to test in an egg drop. Invite them to help the child collect recycled materials to bring to school to use when they create their protective covering, or even invite parents to design and build at home. You can create a STEM family event at school and invite families and children to test their egg-drop contraptions together.

Simple Machines: Pulley

Topic:

Exploring the use of a pulley

Objective:

Children will create a simple machine—
a pulley—using everyday items.

Materials:

Rope

Rolling pin

Nonbreakable object to be attached as a
weight (wooden log, book)

Two child-sized chairs

Overview:

In this whole-group lesson, children help to create a simple machine—
a pulley—and explore how it helps to move heavy objects.

Activity Steps:

1. Talk with the children about what a pulley is and what it can do.
   A pulley is a simple machine that is useful for lifting things. It reduces
   the effort required to raise a load. It consists of a wheel with a
   groove through which a string or rope runs. The rope has a load on
   one end and someone or something pulling at the other end. It can
   be helpful to show some pulleys that they may have seen before—
   for example, a construction pulley on cranes. If your school has a
   flagpole, you can take the children outside to watch as you raise and
   lower the flag with the help of the pulley.

2. Pass around your heavy object, and ask the children to lift it with
   their hands. Talk with them about building a pulley that will make it
   easier to lift the object.

3. Place two child-sized chairs back to back. With the help of a child helper, tie one end of the rope around the rolling pin and attach the other end to the heavy object you will be lifting.

4. Invite two children at a time to use the pulley to lift the object. With your help, they will place one handle of the rolling pin on the top or between the rungs on the chair.

5. Carefully, they can simultaneously turn the rolling pin to wind up the extra rope and lift the object.

6. Talk with the children about which way they felt was easier to lift the object, using the rolling pin or lifting with their hands. Make sure each pair has a chance to use the pulley.

7. Change objects as desired to help the children experience lifting objects of varying weights.

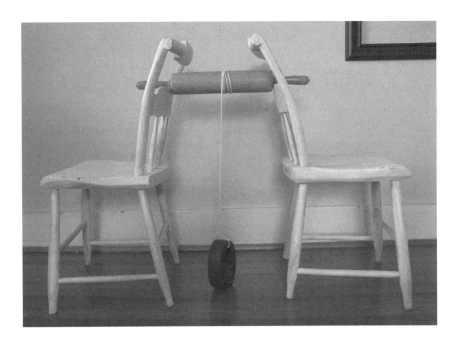

Documentation:

The conversations before, after, and during this whole-group experience will help you to determine the children's levels of understanding and interest in working with pulleys.

Creative Investigations in Early Engineering and Technology

Extension Lesson:

The rolling-pin pulley can be added to the block area or STEM classroom center to encourage the children to continue their exploration. Be sure to provide adult assistance and supervision on the days the pulley is included for children's free exploration.

Straw Gliders

Topic:

Exploring design, air resistance, and balance

Objective:

Children will design and build a straw glider.

Materials:

Clipboard

Paper

Pencils

Plastic or paper drinking straws

Heavy cardstock or 5" x 8" index cards

Tape

Scissors

Creativity Skills:

Exploration

Documentation

Overview:

Children will work individually or alongside others. You will need plenty of space for them to test their gliders.

Activity Steps:

1. Talk with the children about airplanes and paper airplanes, letting them know that today they will have the chance to create a special type of aircraft known as a glider. It can be helpful for the children

to see an example glider or sketched plans for making a glider prior to beginning.

2. Invite them to draw their own glider prior to building; this step is important because it requires them to notice all the parts of the glider and allows them to think about how they may make their gliders unique.

3. To begin building, the children will need to cut the card stock, index card, or stiff paper into separate pieces that measure about 1" x 8" and 1" x 6". The back hoop should be larger than the front hoop to help support and steady the plane in flight.

4. Tape the pieces of paper together into a loop, and tape the paper loops to the ends of the straw with the straw resting on the inside of the loops.

5. Invite the children to hold the straw in the middle with the loops on top (straw at the bottom) and throw it in the air.

6. Once children have experience making one glider, they will be able to create others. Encourage them to be creative with their gliders, paying particular attention to their additions and modifications with your questioning. Which glider flew longest? Why do you think that? Why did that glider crash straight to the ground? What do you think you could change to help it fly longer?

Documentation:

The children's draft drawings and built gliders can serve as documentation of their understandings of this test-flight design process.

Extension Lesson:

Create an airplane station in your classroom with sample plans for building both paper and straw airplanes. A great resource for paper airplane templates can be found at http://www.foldnfly.com/

Simple Machines: Wheels Everywhere

Topic:

Exploring the use of wheels and axles

Objective:

Children will identify various wheels and axles found in their everyday environment.

Materials:

Clipboard

Paper

Pencils

Colored pencils, crayons, markers, or watercolor paints

An example wheel and axle (3" paper circle with a hole in the center for a pencil to act as an axle)

> **Creativity Skills:**
>
> Exploration
>
> Documentation

Overview:

In this introductory lesson, children will locate wheels and axles in their everyday environment and document those findings.

Activity Steps:

1. Show children an example wheel and axle, and talk with them about the wheels they see every day. Many children will be familiar with wheels but may never have seen how an axle and wheel work together as a simple machine.

2. Using your example, show children how the axle and wheel work together to move objects. Invite the children to take turns exploring your example.

3. Talk with the children about going on a walk today to look for wheels and axles; they will use their clipboards with paper to draw what they find on their walk.

4. On your walk together, take the time to talk with the children about their findings and encourage them to find additional wheels and axles to compare.

5. Ask questions, such as, "What do you notice about the size of the wheels on that bicycle compared to the size of the wheels on that truck?" or "Why do you think that cars have smaller wheels than buses?" These types of guided-inquiry questions can support their thinking and provide opportunities for you to gauge their understandings.

6. When children return to the classroom, explain that they can use colored pencils, crayons, markers, or watercolor paints to continue illustrating their wheel and axle drawings.

Documentation:

The children's draft drawings and final illustrations can serve as documentation of their understandings and the exploratory walk.

Extension Lesson:

Explore the everyday environment for examples of all six of the classical simple machines—lever, pulley, inclined plane, wedge, screw, and wheel and axle.

Group Exploration Games:

Push or pull—Identifying the force: Mime or mimic movements such as pulling open a door or pushing a toy away from you, and have the children identify and label the correct force. As children gain experience with the game, invite them to create a movement for their classmates to identify.

Feet to feet, hand to hand—Feeling a push, feeling a pull: Children will play in pairs and will sit facing each other. They will place the soles of their feet or the palms of their hands together and take turns pushing against the other. To experience a pull, have each child hold onto a short rope and take turns gently pulling on the rope while sitting down.

Children's Books

Beaty, Andrea. 2013. *Rosie Revere, Engineer*. New York: Abrams Books for Young Readers.

With beautiful watercolor and pen-and-ink illustrations and rhyming verse, *Rosie Revere, Engineer* provides a timeless story of the trials and tribulations of engineering design and exploration from a child's perspective.

Llewellyn, Claire. 2004. *And Everyone Shouted, Pull!: A First Look at Forces and Motion*. North Mankato, MN: Capstone Young Readers.

Part of the First Look: Science series, this book introduces children to the concepts of force and motion through a fun tale of animals working together to push and pull a cart.

Stille, Darlene R. 2004. *Motion: Push and Pull, Fast and Slow*. North Mankato, MN: Capstone Young Readers.

Using examples from everyday life—swinging, playing soccer, a crawling baby—this book provides detailed information to help children explore the concepts of motion by learning about movement, speed, force, and inertia.

2

Engineering Design: Sound, Light, and Shadow

Understanding Sound

The sounds we hear are caused by the emission of energy in the form of a vibration—sounds are made when something vibrates. A *sound wave* is a pressure wave that displaces particles of air as it passes through them. The sound wave vibrates in the direction of travel, and the amplitude (*volume*) and frequency (*pitch*) of the sound wave depends on what the source is and the amount of energy supplied outward. Sounds can be loud or soft (*amplitude*) and high or low (*frequency*).

Understanding Light and Shadow

Light is a form of energy and travels as a particle and as a wave. Most objects don't make their own light but rather reflect or absorb light. A person can see light in seven different colors—violet, indigo, blue, green, yellow, orange, and red. An object will appear to us as different colors based upon what colors it reflects. The children in your classroom will be most familiar with the sources of light they encounter on an everyday basis—the sun, household or classroom lighting, flashlights, and the light tables or projectors in your classroom. Building your lessons around their everyday experiences with light will help to make the concept of light and shadow personally relevant for each child.

Building off of the understanding of light, light sources, and color, shadows are the result of natural light or electrical light blocked by an object. Every shadow needs both a light source and an object to form the shadow. The object can block all or part of the light, which will result in variations of the shapes of shadows. The size of shadows will also vary based upon their relative proximity to the light source—the shadows made as a child walks across a paved parking lot differ as the child walks into school at 8:00 a.m. or as she leaves at noon.

Another component to the science of shadows and light is the understandings of why some objects block all, part, or none of the light source, while others reflect light. Objects that block all of the light are known as *opaque*—you can't see through these objects. Objects that let part of the light through are known as *translucent*; these objects act as filters and only allow certain colors of light through. *Transparent* objects, such as clear glass windows, let all of the light pass through. Finally, *reflective* objects redirect light and do not let light pass through. Your students may be most familiar with the reflective lights placed on their bicycles or bicycle helmets.

There will be many natural opportunities that emerge throughout the day that will allow you to promote a range of engineering and design experiences with sound, light, and shadow. As with any STEM topic, it is best to begin with the most naturalistic experiences, using materials that are familiar to your students, and gradually scaffold their experiences and use of science equipment as they gain knowledge and show additional interest in the topic. As you plan activities involving sound, light, and shadow, consider the guidance from the related *Next Generation Science Standards* from the National Academies Press. While these standards are written to guide K–12 learning experiences, the disciplinary core ideas they are based upon can be a helpful guide for preschool engineering and design experiences as you work to help build children's foundational knowledge and creative thinking skills.

Wave and Light Properties

Sound can make matter vibrate, and vibrating matter can make sound.

Objects can be seen if light is available to illuminate them or if they give off their own light.

Some materials allow light to pass through them; others allow only some light through; and others block all the light and create a dark shadow on any surface beyond them, where the light cannot reach. Mirrors can be used to redirect a light beam.

Developing Possible Solutions

Designs can be conveyed through sketches, drawings, or physical models. These representations are useful in communicating ideas for a problem's solutions to other people.

Source: NGSS Lead States. 2013. *Next Generation Science Standards: For States, By States*. Washington, DC: The National Academies Press.

Vignette for Understanding: Playing with Light

Mrs. Davis has set up a small light table made from an overhead projector in the science center today, along with a variety of tinted, translucent geometric pieces for her three-year-old students to explore. Noah is carefully arranging the various shapes—octagon, parallelogram, triangle—to make sure that each piece is touching the side of the piece he placed in front of it before sliding the connected shape underneath the illuminated area of the table. As he slides the pieces in to place on the table, he glances up to the wall where his shapes are being projected. With a little adjusting, he seems satisfied with his arrangement as he calls Mrs. Davis over to see what he has created. Mrs. Davis quickly notes the placement of his shapes and how they are so close together that no light is coming through any spaces between shapes. Noah announces that he is going to keep arranging pieces to fill up the illuminated space with shapes. As he works, he glances periodically between the illuminated wall reflecting his shape placement and the light table itself to make decisions that guide his placement choices.

Reflection

As Noah's exploration of light, positive space (translucent shapes), and negative space (space between shapes) demonstrates, sound, light, and shadow are naturally intriguing and engaging topics for young children.

Noah studies shapes at the light table.

These vast concepts can be explored from several different disciplinary perspectives—visual and language arts, science, and engineering design. When an early childhood teacher takes the time to offer scaffolding and guidance through supportive pedagogical practices, such as with Mrs. Davis as she took the time to observe Noah's actions and offer descriptive observations, exploration experiences can turn into experiences where young children experiment, observe, and rework their original designs and ideas. Carefully designed learning experiences with sound, light, and shadow can provide the children in your classroom with creative opportunities to explore, test, and ultimately extend their understandings. Keeping these learning experiences open ended and playful will help to promote a classroom culture that supports inquiry and experimentation.

Sound, Light, and Shadow across the Curriculum: Planning Tips

Interactions with sound, light, and shadow in an early childhood classroom can take place outdoors in natural environments involving the children themselves as part of the environment, as well as involving reclaimed or recycled materials and purchased classroom materials. You can create outdoor lessons to engage children in the spaces around your school and neighborhoods in addition to a STEM center in your classroom. It is important to keep in mind that the experiences you plan indoors with sound will undoubtedly raise the volume of your classroom, so placing those activities away from reading or quiet spaces will be an important consideration to support all the students in your classroom.

Questions for Inquiry and Exploration with Sound, Light, and Shadow

The following are a brief listing of questions that can be used to encourage guided-inquiry explorations with sound, light, and shadow:

- Is the sound you hear quiet or loud, high or low? How do you know that?

- Will the light go through this object, or will the object block it? Why do you think that?

- What objects in this classroom will block light completely? Which will allow some light to pass through?

- How can we tell if light will go through this (object)? What should we do to test to see if light will go through this (object)?

- What color will we see if we shine this flashlight through this (object)? Why do you think that?

Lesson Ideas

Going on a Sound Walk

Topic:

Different objects create different sounds

Every sound has a source that we can trace to find out what object is making a particular sound.

Objectives:

Children will participate in the identification of different everyday sounds.

Children will trace an identified sound to its source.

Materials:

Sound Walk picture page (see page 45)

Clipboards and pencils (for each child)

Audio recorder

| **Creativity Skills:** |
| Exploration |
| Visualization |
| Documentation |

Overview:

Before leaving on the walk, print copies of the Sound Walk picture page or create your own page using images that represent sounds the children are likely to hear on a brief walk. Be sure to leave a place on the page where the children can draw their own sound images; this will challenge them to think (and listen) beyond the images and sounds you've placed on the page.

Activity Steps:

1. Just prior to the walk, talk with the children about the sounds they hear every day. Ask the children questions about their past

experiences with sounds outdoors: "What sounds have you heard when we are outside on the playground?" "Can you think of what makes ___ sound?" "When you go on a walk near your home, what are some of the sounds you hear?" Let the children know that they are going to go on a special sound walk.

2. Share the Sound Walk picture page with students and ask them if they can connect a sound to each image—for example, a picture of tree leaves blowing is a picture that identifies the sound of wind.

3. Be sure that each child has a clipboard, pencil, and the Sound Walk picture page to record their sound observations.

4. Invite the children to be very quiet on the walk so that everyone is able to concentrate on listening for sounds.

5. Once they identify a sound, they can share with others. Use these sharing moments to connect the idea that sounds can be traced to a source. If they hear a dog's bark, that means that a dog is close enough to see and for them to find.

6. Use your audio recorder to record sounds heard on the walk. This recording can be used once you are back in the classroom to revisit and extend the experience.

Documentation:

The children's Sound Walk pages can serve as a form of documentation. Anecdotal notes taken during the walk can also help to identify which sounds children were able to connect back to their source.

Extension Lesson:

To extend this experience to areas beyond walking distance of your school, use an audio recorder to record novel sounds. Play these back to your students as a whole group so that they can work together to identify the sources of the sounds. You can deepen the complexity of the experience by adding in the concepts of volume (loud and soft) and pitch (high and low) during the walk. You can also invite the children to create their own Sound Walk picture page to use on a walk in the future.

Going on a Sound Walk

Circle the pictures of the items you heard.

Draw your own sound picture:

Print one copy for each student of the sample Sound Walk picture page.

Class Band: Creating Instruments

Topic:

Different objects create different sounds.

Sound can make matter vibrate, and vibrating matter can make sound.

Objectives:

Children will participate in the creation of simple instruments.

Children will play their created instruments and notice the sounds made from vibrations.

Teacher note: Build one of each instrument ahead of time, so the children can see and play the examples.

Materials for creating drums:

Small tin cans (Cover any sharp edges with duct tape.) or cylindrical cardboard containers (for example, oatmeal or raisin containers)

Paint or markers to decorate the drum (optional)

20" balloons, one per can

Scissors

Ribbon or fabric

Craft glue or hot glue (Hot-glue gun is for adult use only.)

> **Creativity Skills:**
>
> Exploration
>
> Visualization
>
> Strategic planning
>
> Opportunities for unique problem solving

Instructions for creating a drum:

Place the balloon over the open end of the can or container. Adding a strip of ribbon or fabric with glue around the edge of the balloon can help it stay in place. Encourage the child to personalize her instrument with the paint or markers.

Materials for creating a kazoo:

Cardboard tube (paper-towel roll, cut in half)

Wax paper (3" x 3" square)

Rubber band

Sharp pencil (or other sharp object, adult use only)

Paint or markers (optional)

Instructions for creating a kazoo:

Adult: Use the pencil or other sharp object to make a small hole about 2 inches from one end of the cardboard tube. Child: Place a square of wax paper over the end of the cardboard tube nearest the hole you've created, and secure by wrapping a rubber band around tightly. Encourage the child to personalize her instrument with the paint or markers.

Materials for creating a straw flute:

8 plastic drinking straws

Masking tape

Scissors

A ruler

Pen or pencil

Paint or markers (optional)

Instructions for creating a straw flute:

Start by cutting the first straw to 8 inches in length. Each straw you cut will be a half inch shorter than the previous one (8, 7.5, 7, 6.5, 6, 5.5, 5, 4.5). Line up the straws from longest to shortest with the uncut ends all at the same height, and tape them together. Use two bands of tape to hold the flute together for strength. Encourage the child to personalize her instrument with the paint or markers.

Overview:

Children will work in small groups to each create an instrument.

Activity Steps:

1. As a whole group, ask the children to hum along to a favorite class song. As they hum, show them how to gently press their fingers against their necks. What can they feel? Introduce the term *vibrations* to the students and talk briefly about sounds caused by vibrations.

2. Talk about other examples of sounds they may have seen or felt to reinforce their understandings of vibrations. Show them examples of the three instruments—drum, kazoo, and straw flute—and invite them to think about which instrument they would like to build.

3. It's best to invite children to create their instruments in a small group, as they will need assistance. To help them make an informed choice about which instrument to create, invite the children to play all three of the instruments, reinforcing the idea of vibration and sound.

4. Once they are ready to construct their instruments, work with each child to build the instrument together using the aforementioned instructions. Invite the child to be actively involved in the creation of the instrument. Keep your sample instruments within reach so that the child has an idea of what she will be working toward as she builds her instrument.

5. As you work, prompt the child with questions to think about the role of vibration in the sounds of her instrument.

    - Why do we need the balloon to stretch tightly across the top of the container?

    - Why do you think we need to punch a hole in the tube for the kazoo?

    - What will be the difference when you blow into the long straw and the short straw?

6. Once everyone has created instruments, invite the class to play together, and have the children trade instruments to experience new sounds.

Documentation:

Take anecdotal notes during the process of building and playing with the instruments, which will serve to provide information on the children's understandings.

Extension Lesson:

Engage the children in the process of making additional instruments to play with the idea of sound and vibration. Additional ideas for instruments can include a paper-plate tambourine (with dried beans inside); plastic bottle shakers (with beans, plastic beads, or rice inside); or a box guitar (with strings).

Outdoor Reclaimed-Materials Sound Wall

Topic:

Different objects create different sounds.

Sound can make matter vibrate, and vibrating matter can make sound.

Every sound has a source that we can trace to find out what object is making a particular sound.

Objectives:

Children will trace an identified sound to its source.

Children will participate in the creation of the sound wall.

Children will play the sound wall and notice the differing sounds made from the different materials.

Materials:

Reclaimed kitchen items—pots, pans, potato mashers, wooden and metal spoons, wire whisks, muffin tins, metal cooling racks (used for baking), and cake pans

Clipboards, paper, and pencils

Zip ties, metal hooks, and wood screws

Outdoor fence or location where reclaimed items can be placed

Creativity Skills:

Exploration

Visualization

Documentation

Opportunities for unique problem solving

Strategic planning

Overview:

This is a long-term project that will involve the children in the planning, design, building, and experimentation phases. You can also involve families in the process of materials gathering and building.

Activity Steps:

1. Explain to your students what an outdoor sound wall is and how one can be created out of everyday items that are no longer being used. This is a great project to introduce in connection to studies of the environment and recycling/reusing materials.

2. The next step of the project is to collect items that can be used to create a sound wall. If you'd like to involve families in the process, work with the children to create a wish list of items, and send a letter home explaining the project.

3. Once materials have been collected, the next step in the process is designing the sound wall. Have the children play with the materials and think about the sounds that can be created on their sound wall.

4. Invite the children to help locate a place outdoors (along a fence will work best). Introduce the children to the idea of sketching a plan for the wall by creating a sketch (See the photo on page 51.)

5. Lay out the materials the class has gathered, and encourage each child to sketch a plan for the wall.

6. Once all sketches are completed the class can select a sketch (or two) that captures the elements most desired in the sound wall.

7. Using metal hooks, screws, or zip ties, attach the items to the wall according to plan. Keeping the items moveable or interchangeable will help maintain children's interest in the wall over time.

8. Once the items are installed, invite the children to create sounds using the collected spoons and whisks.

Documentation:

The children's sketches can serve as a form of documentation along with their activities building and playing the sound wall. Anecdotal notes taken during their play can also help to identify which sounds children were able to connect back to their source.

Extension Lesson:

To extend this experience you can change out the materials on the sound wall. Encourage the children to record the sounds, so that sounds can be replayed once back in the classroom, and the children can try to decipher which item is associated with each sound.

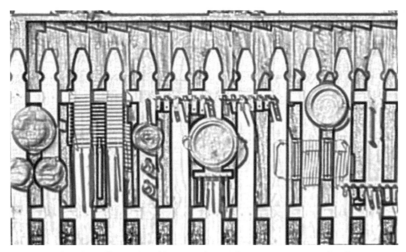

A variety of everyday objects can be used to construct a sound wall.

What Blocks the Light?

Topic:

Some materials allow light to pass through them (transparent), and others act as filters and only allow certain colors of light through (translucent), while others block light completely (opaque).

Objectives:

Children will explore the concepts of *transparent*, *translucent*, and *opaque* everyday items.

Children will group objects by the type of light each is allowing through.

Materials:

Small classroom materials that are transparent, translucent, and opaque (for example, wooden blocks, colored counting bears, translucent counters, transparent counters, and transparent light-table materials)

Light table or projector

Digital camera

Creativity Skills:

Exploration

Visualization

Documentation

Problem solving

Overview:

Children will work individually or in small groups depending on the size of your light table or projector.

Activity Steps:

1. Invite the children to play with the materials you've collected, and ask questions about what they notice about their differences— "What happens to the light when I put this blue counting bear on the light table? Is that different than when I place this clear block on the table?" "What happens to the light when you place the pieces on top of each other?"

2. Be sure to give the children room to explore and interact with the objects in their own ways. During this time, you can also narrate what you are seeing about the relationship between light and objects—"Wow, when you place the two clear pieces together, I can still see the light shining through."

3. As the children are exploring, you can introduce the words and concepts of *transparent*, *translucent*, and *opaque*. Be sure to give the children room to explore and interact with the objects in their own ways.

4. As a final step in their explorations, invite the children to group the objects they believe are alike or different based upon their interaction with light.

5. Be sure to photograph their groupings to document their thinking and explorations.

Documentation:

You can take anecdotal notes on their explorations and play, and the photographs can serve as a final documentation.

Extension Lesson:

It is a good idea to invite children to repeat their play at the light table numerous times, as they will gain greater understanding during additional interactions. You can also invite the children to collect materials that they want to explore at the light table.

Flashlight Colors

Topic:

Some materials allow light to pass through them (transparent), and others act as filters and only allow certain colors of light through (translucent).

Objectives:

Children will explore the concepts of *transparent* and *translucent* using flashlights.

Children will transform their flashlights to allow a chosen color of light through and will work with peers to create new colors.

Materials:

Flashlights (plastic with shatter-free lenses are most appropriate for a preschool classroom)

Colored cellophane or plastic wrap in red, yellow, and blue (or additional colors) in 3" x 3" squares

Rubber bands

Journals or planning pages for students

Colored pencils

Creativity Skills:

Exploration

Visualization

Documentation

Collaboration

Overview:

Children will work in small groups in a darker or limited-light area of the classroom.

Activity Steps:

1. Invite the children to play with the flashlights, and ask questions about what they see reflected in the light—"What color is your flashlight when you shine it on the wall (or ceiling if the wall is not white)?" Prompt them to think about changing the colors of their flashlights by holding pieces of cellophane over the lights. Asking questions or asking them to respond to questions in their journals or planning pages will help them to think about what they know about color and light. Sample journal prompts include: The color I chose to use with my flashlight is _____ (children can write or color in their response). My lesson partners chose to use the colors _____ and _____. What will happen if we mix our colors on the wall? _____

2. The next step is to help the children use the rubber bands to affix the cellophane over the top of their flashlight.

3. Encourage the children to shine their light onto a white ceiling or wall and to overlap their colors with their partners to make new colors and shadows with their modified flashlights.

4. You can introduce the terms *transparent* and *translucent* to the children during their explorations, but focus in on the idea that some materials let all light through and others only allow certain colors through (cellophane).

5. Once they are finished exploring, invite the children to take some time to reflect on the color-mixing experience. Encourage them to show what happened when they overlapped colors in their journals or planning pages.

Documentation:

The children's journals or planning pages can serve as a form of documentation.

Extension Lesson:

Invite the children to engage in shadow play with the modified flashlights. Keeping the flashlights in your science center or in your dramatic play center will support their continued use and exploration in your classroom.

Outdoor Creature-Shadow Drawings

Topic:

Some materials block all the light and create a dark shadow on any surface beyond them.

Objectives:

Children will explore the concept of shadow.

Children will draw a creature using shadows created outdoors.

Materials:

Small plastic animals or creatures

Colored paper

Tray large enough to hold a piece of colored paper

Markers

Overview:

This lesson can be done in small groups or as whole class if you have enough materials.

Creativity Skills:

Exploration

Documentation

Strategic planning

Opportunities for unique problem solving

Activity Steps:

1. Invite the children to select objects to group together on their colored paper/tray and place in the outdoor play space.

2. You can invite the children to move their trays to different areas or check on the trays at different times of day to see if their creature shadows change.

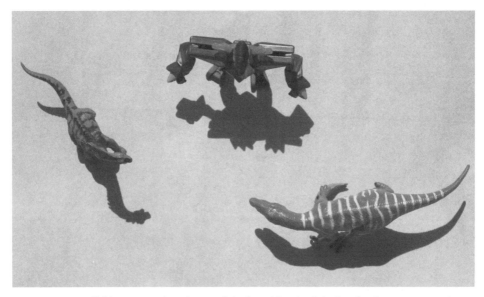

Children can explore the use of shadow with animal-shadow drawings.

3. Once they are happy with their creature shadows, invite the children to carefully trace around the shadows made on their papers. The children can also remove the creatures and work with the traced shadows to add more color and details to their tracings.

Documentation:

The children's shadow tracings can serve as a source of documentation, but also be sure to take anecdotal notes on their observations when they are working at different times of day or in different outdoor areas to modify their creature shadows.

Extension Lesson:

To extend this experience you can invite the children to use sidewalk chalk to trace the shadow of a friend outdoors on a paved area. These tracings can be decorated by others in the class to celebrate the uniqueness of each child and shadow.

Children's Books

Asch, Frank. 2000. *Moonbear's Shadow.* New York: Aladdin Books.

A classic book that invites children to come along as Moonbear tries to outsmart his shadow.

Berge, Claire. 2004. *Whose Shadow Is This?* North Mankato, MN: Picture Window Books.

Whose Shadow Is This? asks children to join in as they explore a variety of different animal shadows of various shapes and sizes, from a hummingbird to a giraffe.

Pfeffer, Wendy. 2016. *Sounds All Around*. New York: HarperCollins.

Sounds All Around invites children to explore how people and animals use different kinds of sounds to communicate, through lively text and colorful illustrations.

Showers, Paul. 1993. *The Listening Walk*. New York: HarperCollins.

The 1993 edition is an updated version of the 1960s classic with colorful and engaging illustrations. *The Listening Walk* encourages children to slow down and pay attention to the variety of sounds that can be heard every day.

3

Engineering Design: The Built Environment and Construction

Construction and building are favorite experiences for many young children. When we explore the built environment through the lens of engineering design, we can build upon children's natural interests and take them in new directions. Engineering design is an iterative decision-making process that requires knowledge of the sciences, mathematics, and the arts. The design process involves several different steps (identifying the problem, collection of basic design data, design work, preparation of plans, and construction), which you can work to implement in your classroom experiences to varying degrees. For example, integrating the idea of planning is an important concept that can be extended to young children's experiences with building. Sketching a plan of a desired building or scene would require your students to begin slowly as they think through what they want their building to look like, where they are going to construct, and what types of materials are needed to begin. Experiencing planning in an authentic manner will encourage them to engage creatively and cognitively. There are also additional challenges that children will encounter as they work to move their two-dimensional drawings into three-dimensional constructed objects. These are issues of representation and include uprightness, balance, stability, and visual complexity. As children gain experience with the process of design and planning, they will expand their understandings of the built environment.

The following is a list of steps you can introduce your students to as they engage in engineering experiences:

1. Identification of the problem or need: What do we know? What do we need to know or do?

2. Design work: What materials do we have or need? Create sketches or plans.

3. Creation/Construction: Gather needed materials and build.

4. Test and retest: Does the constructed piece work? What modifications could be made? How could it be improved?

5. Revise and rebuild: Gather needed materials and build.

6. Show and share your work: How can you tell or show others what you've created?

As you plan activities involving building and construction, consider the guidance from the related *Next Generation Science Standards* from the National Academies Press. While these standards are written to guide K–12 learning experiences, the disciplinary core ideas that they are based upon can be a helpful guide for preschool engineering experiences as you work to help build children's foundational knowledge and creative-thinking skills.

Core Ideas in Engineering

Structure and Properties of Matter

- Different properties are suited to different purposes.

- A great variety of objects can be built up from a small set of pieces.

Defining and Delimiting Engineering Problems

- A situation that people want to change or create can be approached as a problem to be solved through engineering.

- Asking questions, making observations, and gathering information is helpful in thinking about problems.

- Before beginning to design a solution, it is important to clearly understand the problem.

Developing Possible Solutions

Designs can be conveyed through sketches, drawings, or physical models. These representations are useful in communicating ideas for a problem's solutions to other people.

Optimizing the Design Solution

Because there is always more than one possible solution to a problem, it is useful to compare and test designs.

Source: NGSS Lead States. 2013. *Next Generation Science Standards: For States, By States.* Washington, DC: The National Academies Press.

Vignette for Understanding: Building with Loose Parts

The block area of Mrs. Greenberg and Mr. O'Neil's classroom is bustling with excitement today because the children are in the building phase of their explorations of loose parts. Yesterday the children were able to explore a wide variety of loose-parts boxes that Mrs. Greenberg and Mr. O' Neil put together. Some boxes contained only natural materials (seashells, rocks, sticks, and leaves), while others, such as the box used by Ayden, contained manufactured objects of various sizes, shapes, and colors. Ayden was drawn to a box that contained only objects that were orange. After exploring the loose-parts boxes, the children were asked to think about what they could build out of their selected materials. Using their sketch books, the children each drew plans for a potential building or scene using only the materials within their boxes. Mr. O' Neil notices Ayden is immersed in her drawing. He sits alongside her and asks, "Do you want to tell me about your plan?" Ayden quickly replies, "I'm making an 'Orangie World,'" and points to her plan. Mr. O' Neil looks over Ayden's plans for "Orangie World" and points out that he can see that she's planning to hang a spider off one of her buildings. He asks, "Is Orangie's World scary?" "No!" replies Ayden. "Orangie is the name of the pig. It's her home. The spider is her friend." Mr. O' Neil replies, "Oh, now I see" and encourages Ayden to finish up her plan and begin building when she decides that her plan is complete. As he gets up from Ayden's side, Mr. O' Neil reminds Ayden, "Remember that you can change your plan if you decide you need to when you begin building." Later in the morning, as

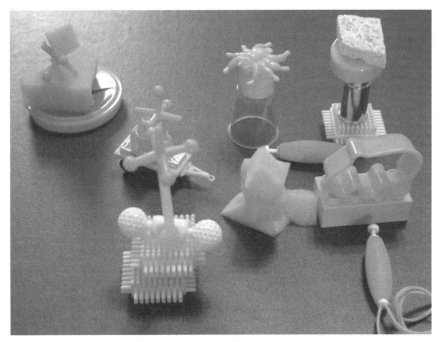

Ayden built "Orangie's World" with loose parts.

Ayden begins to work, shifting her plan into action, she has trouble balancing the spider from the top of the building. She tries a few different solutions—changing buildings, tying string to the spider, laying the spider alongside the edge of the building—but none of those solutions works because the spider keeps falling over. Once again Mr. O'Neil sits beside Ayden and asks her, "Okay, what else could you do to keep the spider in Orangie World? Let's look at your plan. Have you thought about changing the design of one of your buildings?" Ayden looks at her plan and looks back at her buildings. Mr. O'Neil goes on to ask, "Can you make the top of a building flat so that the spider can sit on top?" He and Ayden look through her orange items and find a small cylinder block that has a flat side. Ayden adds the block and tops it with the spider. Grinning, she says, "Now spider and Orangie are together." Mr. O' Neil laughs and tells Ayden that she did a great job thinking about how to balance her buildings.

Reflection

Thinking through design involves opportunities for problem solving and revision, as demonstrated by Ayden's experiences with her spider building. Loose parts and nontraditional building materials can further reinforce opportunities for iterative design because they can be moved, carried, combined, redesigned, taken apart, and put back together in multiple ways. Including loose parts as part of early building and construction explorations promotes children's independent investigations and allows children opportunities to manipulate objects that do not have a singular way to construct or connect. Ayden's experiences creating Orangie World involved cognitive, creative, and self-regulatory skills, which can be a regular occurrence in your classroom when children are provided opportunities to select materials and are encouraged to think through their actions and ideas.

The Built Environment and Construction across the Curriculum: Planning Tips

Experiences with the conceptual ideas behind the built environment and construction can take place every day in your classroom and outdoor play spaces if children are provided with a wide variety of building materials. The possibilities for materials to include in an indoor or outdoor building area are endless: from materials typically used for building (unit blocks, hollow blocks, foam blocks, cardboard blocks) to nontraditional building materials (natural tree blocks, wooden strips and planks, ceramic tiles, small pavers or bricks, stones) and unexpected building materials (clay, natural materials, fabric). Providing children with a rotating variety of materials will help to push their building in new directions. Space is an important consideration because children's constructions may be large and may also not be put away after their time in the space is over. If children are given repeated opportunities to construct and add on to a piece, it will be increasingly more complex over time.

Questions for Inquiry and Exploration in Motion

The following is a brief listing of questions that can be used to encourage creative and design-based explorations with the built environment and construction:

- Did you make a plan for your construction? What materials do you need?

- What would happen if you used a different material? What could you try?

- What can you do to make sure that is balanced?

- Have you walked around your construction to look at it from all sides? What do you notice?

- What do you need to change for your construction to stay together? What can you do differently?

Lesson Ideas

Can You Build a . . . ?

Topic:

Different properties are suited to different purposes.

A great variety of objects can be built up from a small set of pieces.

Objectives:

Children will explore the properties of traditional and nontraditional classroom building materials.

Children will recreate buildings or built objects using available materials.

Materials:

Small and large building blocks

Loose-parts materials (wood planks; cork; plywood; wicker; balsa-wood strips; wooden craft sticks; glass or plastic cabochons of various sizes, colors, and shapes; stones; and tiles of various sizes and shapes)

Pictures or drawings of buildings, bridges, and transportation vehicles

Creativity Skills:

Opportunities for unique problem solving

Strategic planning

Communication

Collaboration

Digital camera

Overview:

This game will require small groups of children to work together to build a replica of a selected object.

Activity Steps:

1. Explain that the objective of this game is for the group to create a replica of the picture the group chooses together.

2. Invite the children to look through the pictures or drawings you've gathered and agree on which to work with. Encourage the group to look through the materials and talk about which materials will work best for their structure.

3. As they build, remind the children to look back at their picture and then to carefully look at their structure to see if there is anything

that can be modified. If the structure falls or collapses, the group can begin again.

4. Be sure to take a photograph of the final structure.

Documentation:

Take anecdotal notes about the children's ability to collaborate, solve problems, and recognize how to use a variety of materials. The photograph of the constructed piece can be also be used as documentation.

Extension Lesson:

You can promote reflection by displaying the photographs of the children's structures side by side with the pictures they used to inspire their building. Encourage the children to talk about what they see as the same and different between the images. Engage them in a discussion of why they chose to use particular materials.

Making Your Own Bricks

Topic:

Different properties are suited to different purposes.

A great variety of objects can be built up from a small set of pieces.

Objective:

Children will participate in the creation of DIY bricks and will use those bricks in outdoor building experiences.

Materials:

Ice-cube trays or small molds in variety of sizes and shapes (flexible silicone trays will be easiest to release the bricks when dry)

Mud and/or a sand-mud mix

Small buckets and stirrers for mixing

Creativity Skills:

Exploration

Visualization

Solution finding

Digital camera

Towels

Overview:

This lesson is going to take place over several days and is best to do during warm weather so that the bricks dry thoroughly before use.

Activity Steps:

1. Talk with the children about different types of building materials, and ask them to think about the types that they see every day. Let the children know that they will be working in pairs to make mud or sand bricks.

2. Invite the children to choose an ice-cube tray that they will fill.

3. Once outside, encourage the children to mix the mud/sand carefully with water. It will work best if the mixture isn't too wet or too dry—the consistency of toothpaste will create the strongest bricks. This will be messy, so be ready with towels for the cleanup!

4. Let the children fill their ice-cube trays and set them in the sun to dry. Once all of the bricks have dried, work with the children to carefully release them from the molds.

5. Encourage the children to build with their new bricks. Be sure to move the bricks to a covered space when not in use, to preserve them for as long as possible.

Documentation:

This experience can be documented with anecdotal notes on the children's abilities to collaborate and problem solve. The brick-making and building processes can be documented through photos.

Extension Lesson:

To extend this experience, show children photographs of buildings created with other natural materials. Adobe structures will most closely match the experience of the children. You can also encourage the children to add in other natural elements to their building with the mud/sand bricks—small wood pieces or sticks are an easy and accessible addition.

Design Challenge: Building Bridges

Topic:

A great variety of objects can be built up from a small set of pieces.

Before beginning to design a solution, it is important to clearly understand the problem.

Designs can be conveyed through sketches, drawings, or physical models. These representations are useful in communicating ideas for a problem's solutions to other people.

Because there is always more than one possible solution to a problem, it is useful to compare and test designs.

Objective:

Pairs of children will participate in the creation of bridges.

Materials:

Playdough or soft modeling clay

Craft sticks

Straws cut to various lengths between 6 and 2 inches

Sketch paper or journal pages

Pencils

Small plastic animal (cow, dog, horse, or even a dinosaur will work!)

Pictures of bridges to use as inspiration

Creativity Skills:

Exploration

Visualization

Solution finding

Collaboration

Overview:

In this lesson, the children will be undertaking the design challenge of creating a bridge that can be used to move an animal from one side of a river to the other.

Activity Steps:

1. Begin by reading the following challenge statement to the children (or create your own): Johnnie the cow (horse, dog, or dinosaur) got separated from his family. He is on one side of the river, and his family is on the other. Johnnie needs you to create a bridge to help him get across the river to his family. Can you work with a partner to create a bridge that will support Johnnie as he walks across it over the river?

2. Show the children the materials they will be using to build their bridges, as well as the sample bridge pictures, to get them started thinking about their bridge designs. Let the children know that the playdough or clay can be used to connect pieces together.

3. Invite them to sketch out possible designs and share ideas with their partners. Once the pair decides on a design, they can get to work building.

4. Encourage the pair to test the strength and stability of their bridge as they build. They may need to work through several rounds of building and redesign over the course of several days.

5. Once the children's bridge is complete (and the playdough hardened) each pair can test their bridge by placing Johnnie on it.

6. Encourage the children to talk about the differences and similarities they see across the different designs.

Documentation:

The children's design sketches and final bridges can serve as documentation of their thinking and working within the design process.

Extension Lesson:

Additional design challenges can include creating buildings or moving transportation vehicles using a wide variety of materials.

Which Shape Is the Strongest?

Topic:

Different properties are suited to different purposes.

A situation that people want to change or create can be approached as a problem to be solved through engineering.

Asking questions, making observations, and gathering information are helpful in thinking about problems.

Objective:

Children will participate in a group design experiment to test which paper structure shape is the strongest.

Materials:

Card stock or thick paper strips. To create shapes that are similar in size, you will need 6" x 2" strips for the triangles, 6.5" x 2" strips for the cylinders, and 8" x 2" for the cubes.

Clear tape

Scissors

Ruler

Pencil

Creativity Skills:

Exploration

Visualization

Cooperation

Overview:

Triangles are the strongest shape because any added force is evenly spread through all three sides. This lesson can be done in a whole-group or small-group setting, and you can vary the degree of student involvement based upon your students' needs; you can measure and cut all strips prior to the lesson or invite the students to help.

Activity Steps:

1. Talk with the children about the types of shapes they've seen used in construction. Let them know that they are going to participate in a design experiment to find out which shape is the strongest.

2. Fold three paper strips into a triangle, cylinder, and a cube (all will be open on two sides). Invite the children to touch each shape and make a guess at which shape will hold a heavy item (book, wooden block, or plank).

   For the triangle, fold the paper into three equal parts and tape together.

   For the cube, fold the paper in four equal parts and tape together.

   For the cylinder, roll the paper on the 6" side in a circle, then tape the ends together.

3. Lay each shape on the floor with an open side facing down and an open side facing up.

4. Invite the children to place the heavy item on each shape, noticing which shape holds the weight. You may need to increase the weight with another heavy item.

5. Once the results are in, talk with the children about why the triangle held more weight than the other two shapes.

6. Repeat the experiment at least one more time to see if the results are the same—this is an important step in the engineering process and will support the children's understandings when they see the same results over and over. Encourage them to make connections to their own experiences building with blocks.

7. Place additional paper shapes in the block area for the children to further explore.

Documentation:

This experience can be documented with anecdotal notes on the children's abilities to make predictions and talk about the results of the experiment.

Extension Lesson:

To extend this experience, create twelve to sixteen of each shape and have the children work in three groups (one shape per group) to create a structure out of their assigned shape that they think will hold the most weight. Encourage them to test their structures prior to the final test in order to make modifications to their design. Test the structures one by one and have the children record the results of the experiment.

Engineering Makerspace

Topic:

A great variety of objects can be built up from a small set of pieces.

Designs can be conveyed through sketches, drawings, or physical models. These representations are useful in communicating ideas for a problem's solutions to other people.

Because there is always more than one possible solution to a problem, it is useful to compare and test designs.

Objective:

Children will participate in an open-ended, self-directed engineering makerspace.

Materials:

The next section includes a list of a wide variety of materials that you could include in an engineering-focused makerspace. Not all materials need to be included at any given time. Carefully observe the children's actions in the space to determine when to add, remove, or introduce new materials.

Creativity Skills:

Exploration

Visualization

Solution finding

Collaboration

Safety equipment and general tools:

Child-sized safety goggles, aprons or smocks, magnifying glasses, scissors, rulers, measuring tape, flashlights, STEM journals, timers, paintbrushes, markers, colored pencils, scales, and child-sized tools (hammers, screwdrivers, pliers)

Engineering/building materials:

Recycled/reclaimed plastic (or nonbreakable) cups, bowls, spoons, craft sticks, pipe cleaners, straws, cardboard tubes of various sizes, small pieces of heavy cardboard or thin wood, masking tape, duct tape, and electrical tape, glue sticks or glue, string, twine, or Velcro strips

Overview:

In this lesson, the children will be working in a center in small groups of two to four children, depending on the size and location of your makerspace.

Activity Steps:

1. Place materials in the space in an organized manner so that children can see what is available to them, and talk with the children about the goals of the makerspace: to be creative, to be inventive, and to try out new ideas.

2. Encourage them to sketch out ideas prior to building so that they can think through which materials they need in their design. Be sure to stress that it is important they only use what they think they will need to ensure that they treat the materials well.

Documentation:

The children's design sketches and final constructions can serve as documentation of their thinking and working within the design process. It would be a great idea to display the children's sketches with their completed constructions to further connect the ideas of planning, design, and building.

Extension Lesson:

The focus of the makerspace will change as you add in different materials. Families can be a great source of help if you take the time to request recycled materials—just be specific on the types of materials you are hoping to add so that their donations match up to the interests of the children and your safety requirements.

Children's Books

Beaty, Andrea. 2007. *Iggy Peck, Architect.* New York: Abrams Books for Young Readers.

Iggy Peck is a second grader who loves building and construction—he makes creations out of every item imaginable. Your students will enjoy hearing about how Iggy's planning and building skills save the class from near disaster!

Gibbons, Gail. 1990. *How a House Is Built.* New York: Holiday House.

A classic book that describes the process used to create a house, your students will learn what surveyors, heavy-machinery operators, carpenters, plumbers, and other workers do to build a house.

Guarnaccia, Steven. 2010. *The Three Little Pigs: An Architectural Tale*. New York: Abrams Books for Young Readers.

Using a familiar story and characters, this version of the three little pigs will introduce your students to the famous architects Frank Lloyd Wright, Philip Johnson, and Frank Gehry. Your students will learn about how each architect has his own style, which they can see reflected in the details of the story line and illustrations.

Spires, Ashley. 2014. *The Most Magnificent Thing*. Toronto: Kids Can Press.

With engaging illustrations, *The Most Magnificent Thing* shares the tale of a young girl as she works through the engineering and design process to create the most magnificent thing. This book will help your students understand why ideas and plans are revised and reworked throughout development.

4
Technology: Knowledge and Innovation

Computers and digital technologies are an important part of the modern world, and children need appropriate exposure to these technologies to understand, communicate, and thrive. Each child encounters computers and digital technologies every day in her environment, from the phone in Dad's pocket to the computer at the doctor's office to the interactive whiteboard in the classroom. In early childhood education, we speak about the many languages of children or the ways in which children communicate their thoughts and ideas—painting, dancing, singing, playing, reading, writing, and so on. In today's technological world we have another language to teach and communicate through: coding. *Coding*, also known as computer programming, is a new genre of literacy that allows you to express your ideas and thoughts. All children need to be exposed to the language of coding to understand and interact knowledgeably with technology. As early childhood teachers, we will need to be familiar with the processes and ideas behind coding. Introductory experiences with coding allow young children to engage in a new way to solve problems, learn mathematics, and gain new language skills in a meaningful and engaging context. Coding involves logical and discrete steps and is very powerful because it allows us to create games, artwork, robotic actions—basically anything you can imagine. Coding also has many elements that mirror written language—it is done in a sequence and involves problem solving, planning, cause and effect—and exposure to these skills in coding can reinforce the same skills when applied to reading.

A great resource for teachers wanting to learn more about coding is Code.org®. Code.org is a nonprofit organization that aims to expand access to computer science. Becoming familiar with coding during the preschool years ensures that young children will have a good foundation to build a deeper understanding of technology as they move through schooling. It also ensures that they will have another language through which to express themselves.

The underlying premise of coding is known as an "if, then, else" statement; this is known as a conditional statement in programming. To begin, you can think of the "if" as a test and the "then" and "else" as a response, such as true or false. The "if" statement evaluates the test and runs the code only if the statement is true—for example, "Cupcakes are yummy." The answer to which is yes or true,

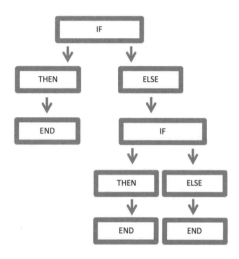

A pictorial representation of "if, then, else"

which is "then," so the code would run. But, let's pretend for a moment that there is someone out there who prefers pie over cupcakes; so, the "if" statement might be "Cupcakes are yummy." The answer to which is no or false, which is "else," and would trigger the "else" condition. The response to "Cupcakes are yummy" can be true "then" or false "else," but it can't be both at the same time. A computer program sends a query to ask if one condition exists, then it commands it to act, based upon the response.

As you plan classroom experiences involving coding, consider the guidance from the International Society for Technology in Education standards for students (ISTE, 2016), which is designed to guide the use of technology in teaching and learning. While these standards are written to guide K–12 learning experiences, the central ideas that they are based upon can be a helpful guide for preschool technology experiences as you work to introduce your students to interactive media. In particular, the central ideas of Empowered Learner, Knowledge Constructor, Innovative Designer, and Computational Thinker are particularly applicable with the use of interactive media in preschool classrooms.

Core Ideas in Technology

- **Empowered Learner:** Students leverage technology to take an active role in choosing, achieving, and demonstrating competency in their learning goals, informed by the learning sciences.

- **Knowledge Constructor:** Students critically curate a variety of resources using digital tools to construct knowledge, produce creative artifacts, and make meaningful learning experiences for themselves and others.

- **Innovative Designer:** Students use a variety of technologies within a design process to identify and solve problems by creating new, useful, or imaginative solutions.

- **Computational Thinker:** Students develop and employ strategies for understanding and solving problems in ways that leverage the power of technological methods to develop and test solutions.

Source: International Society for Technology in Education 2000. *ISTE National Educational Technology Standards.* Eugene, OR: International Society for Technology in Education.

Vignette for Understanding: If, then Fun!

It's a bright and sunny summer day, and Ms. Porter is introducing a new game to her class of five-year-olds called If, Then. "Okay, so remember what we talked about inside. I am the programmer and you are my computers. What does a programmer do?" Jessie excitedly responds, "Tell computers what to do!" "Right," replies Ms. Porter. "Okay, computers, make sure you are facing me and that you can hear me." After the children move into their spaces, Ms. Porter begins the game. "If I jump, you jump, computers," says Ms. Porter. She pauses just for a moment before jumping into the air. The computers in front of her jump, but she notices that some of those computers are jumping more than once. "Wait, wait, wait," she states. "It looks like some of our computers are coded incorrectly. I only jumped one time but some of you jumped a lot. Remember the game is If, Then, and computers respond only to what the programmer has said. Let's try again!" She jumps quickly in the air, and all of her computers jump only one time. "Great!" Ms. Porter exclaims. "Now my computers are getting it." Without saying anything other than *if*, she twirls in a circle and all her computers respond with twirls. The game continues with each child getting a turn to act as the programmer and have the computers repeat her chosen actions.

Reflection

As Ms. Porter's simple game demonstrates, coding can be introduced to young children with or without the use of technology devices. As young children learn through play and movement, it can be very beneficial to introduce an abstract concept such as coding through a concrete game in which the children are actively using their bodies and minds. Ms. Porter's introduction included crucial elements of play, movement, and choice, which will help to engage all children as they learn about new ideas and ways of thinking about the world.

Technology: Knowledge and Innovation across the Curriculum—Planning Tips

As Ms. Porter's game demonstrates, young children do not need to be in front of a computer, tablet, or iPad to begin to learn about how computers and computer games work. It's important to keep in mind the recommendations from NAEYC and the Fred Rodgers Center's

2012 joint position statement, *Technology and Interactive Media as Tools in Early Childhood Programs Serving Children from Birth through Age 8.* They recommend that interactions with technology match with each child's physical, social, emotional, language, and cognitive levels. It is also recommended that young children's interactions with technology and media be playful and support children's opportunities to explore and think creatively.

Questions for Inquiry and Exploration with Technology: Knowledge and Innovation

The following is a brief list of questions that can be used to encourage creative and playful explorations with technology and digital media:

- What do you like about _____ (app or program)?

- Is anything difficult for you when you use _____(app or program)?

- Have you ever played _____(app or program) with a friend? It can be fun to play with someone else.

- What are you most interested in? We can find a game (app or program) to help you learn more about that.

Lesson Ideas

Dramatic Play with Computers

Topic:

The children will explore, through dramatic play, the different ways that computers are used in a variety of settings.

Objectives:

Children will participate in the exploration of settings that involve computer use.

Children will help to research how computers are used by different professionals.

Materials:

The materials you need are dependent upon the type of dramatic play center you set up. Some examples include:

Space Station:

Tables and chairs, computer and keyboard (nonworking or a replica made from boxes), headsets, pictures of the night sky or space, paper, pens, pencils, a large board made to look like command central

Office:

Tables and chairs, computer and keyboard (nonworking or a replica made from boxes), paper, pens, pencils, calculators, phones, cash register

Airport:

Tables and chairs, computer and keyboard (nonworking or a replica made from boxes), paper, pens, pencils, a globe, small pieces of luggage, sample tickets, phone, pictures of faraway locations

Post Office:

Tables and chairs, computer and keyboard (nonworking or a replica made from boxes), paper, pens, pencils, small wrapped boxes, envelopes, calculators, cash register, scanners

Overview:

Children will work together to build a setting to explore how they can use a computer.

Activity Steps:

1. Before setting up a dramatic play center in your classroom, talk with the children about what they know about the theme you plan to introduce. Do they know what happens in a space center for example? What do they think happens?

2. Look at pictures and video together to learn more about the type of work that goes on and how people use computers in that space. For example: If you're making a space center, you can talk about how the computer allows the people in the space center to talk to the astronauts or in a post office how a computer is used to keep track of the packages and letters. Having the children involved in researching the theme will help to enrich their play once they are in the center.

3. Once you have the center set up, be sure to monitor how children are using the materials to determine what you can add or take away from the center to continue to encourage their play and exploration.

Documentation:

As children help you research the center theme, take note of the kinds of questions they are asking and what they notice about the pictures and video they see. You can take photos or videos of the children's play to document their experiences.

Extension Lesson:

Encourage the children to think about the places they've seen computers, and build a dramatic play center around their ideas. This will help to bridge their out-of-school and in-school experiences and allow them to draw upon their own lives.

Coding Games

Topic:

The children will learn about "if, then, else" statements through a series of games scaffolded from least to most complex.

Objective:

Children will participate in an increasingly complex series of "if, then, else" coding games.

Materials:

Nothing is necessary, but you could use a digital camera to document students' game play.

Creativity Skills:

Exploration

Opportunities for unique problem solving

Overview:

You'll want to talk with the children about the role of a computer programmer and how computers, games, and apps work. Often young children think that computer games are more like a movie or TV, so it is important to talk about how the game responds to the ways they play and the buttons they push. Use simple terms and begin with talking about how computer programmers write a series of codes—a special computer language—that determines what happens when you click on something or push a letter or button.

Game 1: If, Then (Version of Monkey See, Monkey Do Game)

Activity Steps:

1. Invite the children to work as a whole group. Choose one child to be the computer programmer and the rest of the children will be computers. In this round of the coding games, the children will do simple see-and-repeat activities.

2. First, the programmer touches her nose, and the computers touch their noses. Remind the children to repeat the programmer's actions exactly as demonstrated and to stop when the programmer stops.

3. Let the programmer continue to model actions. The programmer can call out "if" as she shows her action, and the children can reply with "then" as they repeat the action. Make sure every child has the chance to be both a programmer and a computer.

Activity Steps:

1. Invite the children to work as a whole group, and choose one child to be the computer programmer and the rest of the children will be computers.

2. In this round of the coding games, the children will be doing a more complex activity: the programmer will tell the computers an opposite reaction to her action. For example, the programmer jumps, but the computers walk backwards.

3. As you introduce the game, keep it simple and have the programmer choose only one action/reaction sequence. As the children become more familiar with the game, each programmer can choose two or more sequences, and the children will have to hold those in their memories. For example, "Jump then walk backwards and touch their noses and do jumping jacks."

Documentation:

You can take photos or videos of the children's game play and anecdotal notes of their increasing ability to understand and follow along with the intent of the game.

Extension Lesson:

As children gain experience with the games, you can introduce an "if, then, else" round in which the programmer details two choices for reactions (for example, the programmer touches her toes and computers either twirl (then) or clap (else).

Coding Apps for Preschoolers

Topic:

Self-guided app exploration; empowered learner, knowledge constructor, computational thinker

Objective:

Children will choose and engage with an app that is designed to promote creative interactions with coding.

Materials:

iPad or tablet for children's use with apps loaded

Creative, free apps available for iPad and android platforms include the following:

Creativity Skills:

Exploration

Solution finding

- **Kodable by SurfScore, Inc.** Recommended ages: 4 and up. This app is designed to teach young students to code and will work with prereaders. Children move small fuzz balls through a maze using commands that are introduced during the course of the game.

- **Daisy the Dinosaur by Hopscotch Technologies.** Recommended ages: 4 and up. This app has a simple drag-and-drop interface preschoolers can use to make Daisy move. This app provides a fun introduction to coding.

- **Scratch Jr. by Scratch Foundation.** Recommended ages: 4 and up. This app invites children to snap together virtual programming blocks to make characters move, jump, dance, and sing. Scratch Jr. promotes a creative approach to coding.

- **Cargo-Bot by Two Lives Left.** Recommended ages: 4 and up. This app teaches coding basics through a puzzle game in which the user teaches a robot how to move crates. Young children will appreciate the familiarity of the puzzle concept and the engaging graphics.

Overview:

This lesson works best if children work in pairs to promote collaboration and communication during app play.

Activity Steps:

1. If this is the first time the children are using a particular app, it is a good idea to briefly introduce it and its various functions during whole-group time so that the children have an idea of what the app can do.

2. Invite the pair to choose an app during their time in the technology center. Questions such as, "What happened when you did _____?" "Do you know how to make _____ happen?" and "Why did _____ happen when you did _____?" can help to promote intentionality in their actions.

3. As documentation is an important component of any digital play, ask the children to share their experiences with coding with the class during whole-group time. Children who are particularly interested in coding can also help to explain the app to other children.

Documentation:

Take anecdotal notes about the children's ability to plan, problem solve, and collaborate during explorations.

Extension Lesson:

This lesson can be extended by including an app exploration center as a regular and consistent part of your classroom's activity centers.

Children's Books

Liukas, Linda. 2015. *Hello Ruby: Adventures in Coding.* New York: Feiwel and Friends.

This book follows the adventures of Ruby and her animated friends as they work to solve problems. Through Ruby's approach to problem solving, students will be introduced to the fundamentals of computational thinking—breaking big problems into a series of smaller ones, creating detailed plans, and searching for patterns.

Liukas, Linda. 2017. *Hello Ruby: Journey Inside the Computer*. New York: Feiwel and Friends.

In a follow-up to *Hello Ruby: Adventures in Coding*, this book joins Ruby as she takes a journey into the depths of her father's computer. Students will learn the basic elements of computers and will be challenged to keep their learning going with fun follow-up activities.

Stanley, Diane. 2016. *Ada Lovelace, Poet of Science: The First Computer Programmer*. New York: Simon and Schuster.

Students will be intrigued by the biographic tale of Ada Lovelace, born nearly 200 years before the computer age and credited with developing the first code. The book has beautifully written text and illustrations that will keep young children engaged and interested in learning more about Ada as she grows from an imaginative child to a scientist and mathematician solving problems.

5
Technology: Communication and Collaboration

During the preschool years, young children are developing their understanding of all aspects of the world they live in, which includes many different kinds of digital media and technology. Technology can be an important addition to young children's explorations across the content areas. Just as crayons and markers are used to create and communicate ideas, digital cameras, apps, programs, and digital technologies can be used to support and extend young children's exploration in language and literacy, mathematics, the arts, and sciences.

In a 2012 joint position statement, *Technology and Interactive Media as Tools in Early Childhood Programs Serving Children from Birth through Age 8*, NAEYC and the Fred Rodgers Center recommended that early childhood technology experiences be active, hands-on, engaging, and empowering. Young children's use of digital technologies should also be one of many options to support their learning of new content and new skills. Active engagement is an important consideration of digital-technology use in the classroom, as passive or noninteractive technologies (television, DVDs) are not recommended for use in preschool classrooms because such experiences don't require hands-on, minds-on engagement.

Understanding Communicative and Collaborative Processes with Interactive Media

When we hear the word *technology* we often think of a particular device or gadget that we use in our daily lives. Technology is much more than a particular gadget that helps us to navigate our way around the city or helps us to record and analyze our activity levels throughout the day. Technology invites us to be creative, solve or discover problems, and explore in new ways. Teachers have an important role in modeling appropriate and intentional uses of technology for their students. Being intentional in your adoption and use of technology requires you to have background knowledge and experience using all of the technological tools prior to introducing them to your students. This chapter shares vignettes, lessons, and resources featuring children's engagement with interactive media. Interactive media includes technologies such as software programs, apps, electronic books, digital cameras and video cameras, and some forms of streamed media content that encourages children's collaborative, active engagement. Children's engagement with interactive media should mirror the other types of daily experiences in their lives—playful learning, collaborative learning, sustained exploration, and opportunities to document and share their understanding with others.

The following is a list of questions you can use to help guide the adoption and use of interactive media for student use in the preschool classroom. As you explore and learn from the media prior to sharing it with your students, ask:

* How will this interactive media be used in the classroom?

* Does the interactive media have a distinct purpose, or will it be for general, exploratory use?

* Can the children manipulate the interactive media on their own or with minimal adult assistance?

- Does the interactive media allow the children to do familiar things or engage in novel ways?

- Is the interactive media creating new and different learning experiences for the children?

- Does the interactive media promote play and interaction?

Reflection questions following initial use:

- How do the children use the interactive media, and how well does this use match the original intent?

- Did the children experience any challenges during use? How were these overcome?

- Was the children's interest in the interactive media sustained over time? Did they request to use the media after their initial use?

Carefully consider the arrangement of your classroom workspaces when planning for the use of interactive media. Current research indicates that collaborative technology use with young children has important implications for young children's learning and development. As you plan the space where the media will be housed, take care to provide space for children to work together on tasks so that they can talk, share, and explore together.

As you plan classroom experiences involving interactive media, consider the guidelines from the International Society for Technology in Education standards for students (ISTE, 2016), which are designed to guide the use of technology in teaching and learning. While these standards are written to guide K–12 learning experiences, the central ideas they are based upon can be a helpful guide for preschool technology experiences as you work to introduce your students to interactive media. In particular, the central ideas of Communication and Collaboration, Creative Communicator, and Global Collaborator are particularly applicable with the use of interactive media in preschool classrooms.

Core Ideas in Technology

- **Communication and Collaboration:** Students use digital media and environments to communicate and work collaboratively, including at a distance, to support individual learning and contribute to the learning of others.

- **Creative Communicator:** Students communicate clearly and express themselves creatively for a variety of purposes using the platforms, tools, styles, formats, and digital media appropriate to their goals.

- **Global Collaborator:** Students use digital tools to broaden their perspectives and enrich their learning by collaborating with others and working effectively in teams, both locally and globally.

Source: International Society for Technology in Education 2000. *ISTE National Educational Technology Standards.* Eugene, OR: International Society for Technology in Education.

Vignette for Understanding: Tulips in the Spring

Mrs. Barnes's students gather anxiously around a small garden outside their classroom. The children are excited to see if the Red Emperor tulip bulbs they planted earlier in the year have started to peek through the garden dirt. Mrs. Barnes and her students are participating in a project that spans the northern hemisphere with the goal of tracking the emergence of spring in a scientific way. The project is coordinated by Annenburg Learner's Journey North and is called the Journey North Tulip Test Gardens (www.learner.org/jnorth/tm/tulips/AboutSpring.html). Earlier in the fall, the class planted ten Red Emperor tulip bulbs in a small garden space outside of their classroom, following the guidelines from the project. The project asks students to make and record careful observations of their tulips and report that information to the project via the website in order for all students and classrooms to explore the relationships among climate, location, and the arrival of spring. The students record the growth of the tulips using the Tulip Project page and then upload that data to the Journey North website.

The children excitedly note that several of their tulips have green leaves poking up through the soil. "Okay, kids, let's count how many tulips we can see today," says Mrs. Barnes as she leans down to point at each bunch of green leaves. "One, two, three, four," says the class as they count along with Mrs. Barnes. "Wow, we can see the leaves of four tulips. What do you need to write on your journal page? How many tulips have emerged today?"

TULIP PROJECT	
_____ The tulips are below the ground today	
_____ The tulips have emerged!	
They are _____ tall	
They are _____ color	
My observation:	What I think I will see next:

As the children take the time to write the number four, Mrs. Barnes invites the children to draw their observations of the tulips. Barron was chosen to measure the height of the tulips for additional documentation. As he bends down to measure the tallest tulip, the children watch carefully as he places a ruler alongside the plant. Today the tallest tulip measures 3 inches, and the children carefully record that number in their science journals. Before going inside, Mrs. Barnes asks the children to think about what they will see next week when they make their next observation. How many tulips will they see? She takes the time to invite the children to sit down and draw their observations. Once back inside, Mrs. Barnes and the students sit together as she records the day's observations on the Journey North website. Each participating class has its own dot on the Journey North map, and the children are excited to see their dot change colors, demonstrating that the emergence of spring is occurring at their school site. Mrs. Barnes prints out a few copies of the Journey North maps to put into the science area, along with tulip bulbs, magnifying glasses, and the children's science journals, for further exploration.

Tulips bloom in the students' garden.

Reflection

As the students measure the growth of the tulips, they are exploring how climate and location can affect their garden. The comparisons they are able to draw from the Journey North website will further their understanding of the variables that can slow or increase the growth of living plants.

Lesson Ideas

Topic:

Self-guided app exploration

Objective:

Children will choose and engage with an app that is designed to promote creative explorations.

Materials:

iPad or tablet for children's use with apps loaded

Creative, free apps available for iPad and Android platforms include:

Creativity Skills:

Exploration

Solution finding

- **Draw and Tell by Duck Duck Moose.** Recommended ages: Preschool and up. This app allows children to choose from a variety of different backgrounds, characters, and objects to create drawings. Children can also record a story while they manipulate the characters in their drawings.

- **Kids Doodle: Movie Kids Color & Draw by Bejoy Mobile.** Recommended ages: Preschool and up. This app allows children to choose from more than twenty different brush styles, such as a rainbow brush, crayon brush, and an oil brush. Once children create their drawings, they can employ the video mode to play back the steps they took while creating their drawing, allowing a look into the creation of their artwork step by step.

- **MoMA Art Lab by the Museum of Modern Art.** Recommended ages: Preschool and up (preschoolers will benefit most from the drawing and creation applications). This app allows children to create works of art as they play with color, shapes, and lines. More sophisticated aspects of the app, with which young children will need adult guidance, allow children to create sound compositions, create group drawings, and learn about works of art at MoMA and the artists who created them.

- **Magic Piano by Smule.** Recommended ages: Preschool and up. This app will encourage children to use their fingers to play a keyboard to create their own versions of well-known and contemporary songs.

- **Drawing Desk: Draw, Paint, Doodle, & Sketch by 4 Axis Solutions.** Recommend ages: Preschool and up. This app features four modes for play—Kids Desk, Doodle Desk, Sketch Desk, and Photo Desk. The Kids Desk mode is best suited to young children, as it allows them to use a variety of stamps, brushes, stencils, and stickers to create. Children with experience taking photographs can use the Photo Desk mode to edit and manipulate their digital photographs.

Overview:

Children will work in pairs to promote collaboration and communication during app play.

Activity Steps:

1. If this is the first time using a particular app, it is a good idea to briefly introduce the app and its various functions during whole-group time so that the children have an idea of what a particular app can do. Invite the pair to choose an app to create with during their time in the technology center. Questions such as, "How did you decide to use that type of brush?" "Do you know what _____ does?" and "What can it help you to do?" can promote intentionality in their explorations.

2. As documentation is an important component of any digital play, ask the children to choose an image or two from their work to share with the class or to place in their work portfolios.

Documentation:

Take anecdotal notes about the children's ability to plan, problem solve, and collaborate during explorations.

The children's own images can also serve as a source of documentation.

Extension Lesson:

This lesson can be extended by including an app exploration center as a regular and consistent part of your classroom's activity centers.

Children's work is illustrated on the MoMA Art Lab app.

Tinkering Together

Topic:

Explore the ins and outs of recycled technological devices

Objective:

Children will deconstruct recycled technological devices to explore the many components of the devices.

Materials:

Recycled devices (remote controls, cameras, phones, keyboards, computers, small kitchen appliances)

Hand tools (variety of screwdrivers, pliers)

Small plastic, Styrofoam, or paper trays

Sketch paper and pencils

Overview:

This lesson involves small parts and the use of tools, so please use caution and supervise the children throughout this experience. This lesson works best if children work in pairs so that there is adequate access to needed materials and cooperation with a peer. Often one child will need to hold an object while another child removes screws.

Creativity Skills:
Exploration
Visualization
Solution finding
Strategic planning
Collaboration
Documentation

Activity Steps:

1. In advance of introducing your students to the tinker station, you will want to remove external coverings of these devices or loosen screws, nuts, and bolts to make the tinkering process easier for your students. This will be especially helpful if they are new to using tools. Take care to remove any batteries, including button-sized batteries or other dangerous components.

2. Invite the children to work together to take apart any of the devices you have available. Instruct them to place all deconstructed pieces into the trays available on their worktable.

3. While the children are working, it can be helpful to ask them to think about what a particular part of the device does. Asking, "What do you think that part of the phone does?" and "Why do you think that?" can encourage them to think about the many pieces they are uncovering.

4. As part of the process, invite the children to take the time to sketch the "insides" of their devices. These sketches can be used later in extension activities and for documentation of the learning experience.

Documentation:

Take anecdotal notes about the children's ability to problem solve and collaborate during deconstruction.

The children's drawings can serve as an additional a source of documentation.

Extension Lesson:

This lesson should be extended into a building phase once children have deconstructed the available devices. They can use the component parts to create a recycled object; their sketches of the deconstruction experience can serve as the beginning of sketching a recycled creation.

Where in the World?

Topic:

Using digital media to communicate and work collaboratively at a distance

Objective:

The children will digitally follow a peer or teacher on his travels and identify his location on a map, tracking his location over time.

Materials:

iPad or tablet with Google Maps and Google Earth installed

Sketch paper and pencils

Printout of a state, province, your country's, or a world map

Creativity Skills:

Exploration

Visualization

Collaboration

Communication

Documentation

Overview:

Children will work together as a whole class with teacher guidance so that there is adequate access to needed materials and assistance with typing location information. Whole-group time or circle time would be an appropriate setting for this experience. Prior to beginning this lesson, you will need to arrange with a student's family or fellow teacher who is traveling to check in with you every day to share his location. It can be helpful for the traveler to also share pictures of the trip each day for the children to use in the lesson as well.

Activity Steps:

1. To begin the group experience, talk with the children about maps and how they've previously used maps.

2. Remind them that a classmate or teacher is currently traveling and that they are going to follow along with his travels by finding the traveler's location on a map. Each day, use Google Maps or Google Earth to explore the day's location, and invite a child to mark the location on the printed map.

3. Invite children to use their sketch paper and pencils to create their own maps or draw pictures of the photos they've seen or explored on Google Earth of the location.

4. Be sure to use the map to anchor back to the school's location each day to orient the children to their own location.

Documentation:

The class map with marked locations can serve as a point of documentation and reflection for the children, so be sure to hang it at the children's eye level.

Extension Lesson:

This lesson can be extended by inviting the traveler to class, once his trip has ended, to share more information about the trip and for the children to share their maps and drawings.

Virtual Field Trip

Topic:

Using digital media to explore the informal learning environments from around the globe

Objective:

The children will use the internet to virtually explore a museum or zoo.

Materials:

iPad or tablet for the children's use (must have internet access)

Websites to Visit

Boston Children's Museum—Collections
http://www.bostonchildrensmuseum.org/exhibits-programs/collections

The Field Museum—Research and Collections
https://www.fieldmuseum.org/science/research

Monterey Bay Aquarium—Live Web Cams
https://www.montereybayaquarium.org/animals-and-experiences/live-web-cams

Museum of Modern Art—Destination Modern Art
http://www.moma.org/interactives/destination

National Gallery of Art—Art Zone
http://www.nga.gov/kids/zone/zone.htm

The Smithsonian Museum of Natural History—Tours and Images
http://naturalhistory.si.edu/VT3/list.html

Zoo Atlanta—Panda Cam
http://www.zooatlanta.org/1212/panda_cam

Creativity Skills:

Exploration

Collaboration

Communication

Overview:

This lesson works best initially as a whole-group experience so that the children learn how to look at a website and click through a virtual exploration. As they gain experience, you can locate a particular virtual site for them to explore and ask children to work in pairs. Be sure to explore the website you are going to have available for student use ahead of time, so that you can be certain the content is appropriate for your students.

Activity Steps:

1. Ask the children if they've ever been to a museum or zoo. What do they remember most about their experience? Were the museums or zoos local or far away? Let the children know that many museums and zoos have websites where you can take a virtual trip without leaving the classroom.

2. Choose a website and take the time to explore the virtual trip components with the children. Be sure to pause and ask questions just as you would if you were on a field trip.

   - What do you notice about this object? Do you think it's big or small?

   - What colors do you see in this painting?

   - How old do you think the panda bear is? Why do you think that?

3. Once children move to exploring in pairs, periodically check in with them about their virtual experiences. It is a good idea to ask the children to report back to the whole class about what they experienced on their virtual trip and even share an image or two that they found interesting.

Documentation:

Take anecdotal notes about the children's ability to explore, problem solve, and collaborate during their virtual trip.

Extension Lesson:

This lesson works best when you combine the content of the virtual field trips with other explorations in the classroom. For example, a virtual tour of the objects housed at the National Air and Space Museums (https://airandspace.si.edu/collections/collections-on-display) can supplement other lessons related to transportation or space.

Collaborative Storytelling: What We Did!

Topic:

Using technology to facilitate group storytelling

Objectives:

Children will use digital media to communicate and work collaboratively.

Children will use digital media to communicate clearly and express themselves verbally and visually.

Materials:

Free online programs include:

- Prezi, a cloud-based program: https://prezi.com/

- Animoto, an online video creation program: https://animoto.com/

- Kizoa, an online program where you can make slideshows, videos, and animated collages: https://www.kizoa.com/.

Creativity Skills:

Exploration

Communication/ Collaboration

Documentation

Safety note: Be sure to password protect or set the privacy settings to *secure* for any online site used, in order to protect the images and children in your classroom.

Digital copies of photos of class activities that the students can use

Overview:

Introduce the concept of a group storytelling experience in your whole-group time.

Activity Steps:

1. Talk with the children about how they will work together to create a story. If this is a first-time experience, it can help the children to begin with a familiar story and modify it as the activity moves along. Stories about recent class activities such as a field trip, class project, or party provide an easy starting point because they involve shared experiences with which all your students can relate.

2. Following the choice of the story line, introduce the children to the program you have chosen for use in this activity.

3. Share photos with the class, and invite the children to recall the activity pictured in the photos. Choose one photo to begin the story, and ask the class to narrate the text while you type the beginning of the story.

4. Have the children work in pairs to select a photo and type the accompanying text. A teacher will need to offer support in the spelling of the text, but encourage the children to take turns typing and dragging the photos into place.

5. Once the class story is complete, be sure to share with families.

Documentation:

Take anecdotal notes about the children's ability to collaborate, problem solve, and visualize.

Group documentation can include the story itself as a means to document the ways in which children expressed their understandings and ideas.

Extension Lesson:

Once children gain initial experience using photos and text to document an experience or story, they can begin to take a role in developing the documentation of class experiences. Encourage your students to create their own documentation pages to put into their portfolios or other forms of classroom documentation. This will help communicate their perspectives to others. Video can also be introduced as a form of collaborative storytelling.

Children's Books

Dyckman, Ame. 2012. *Boy + Bot.* New York: Knopf Books for Young Readers.

This book tells an engaging tale of the adventures of a boy and a robot who meet by happenstance. *Boy + Bot* will help to connect young children to the idea of interacting and communicating with technology—even when they may not understand each other.

Fliess, Sue. 2013. *Robots, Robots Everywhere!* New York: Golden Books.

Colorful robots can be found in locations near and far and will inspire the imagination of every preschooler as they connect to locations in faraway places and to spaces they live in each day.

Tougas, Chris. 2012. *Mechanimals.* Victoria, BC: Orca.

Mechanimals is an exciting tale of creating and tinkering as a farmer needs to create animals on his farm following a tornado. The farmer's creativity stresses the importance of problem solving and resourcefulness by creating animal bots to help out on the farm. Children will be encouraged to think about the ways that technology can help us.

Creative Investigations in Early Engineering and Technology

Index

A

Aerodynamics, 18–19, 33–34
Air resistance
  lesson ideas, 28–30, 33–34
  defined, 16
Aluminum foil, 28
Ambiguity, 6
Amplitude, 38
Android, 94
App exploration, 84–86, 94–96
Applied force, 15
Apps
  Cargo-Bot by Two Lives Left, 85
  Daisy the Dinosaur by Hopscotch
    Technologies, 85
  Draw and Tell by Duck Duck Moose, 94
  Drawing Desk: Draw, Pain, Doodle,
    & Sketch by 4 Axis Solutions, 95
  Kids Doodle: Movie Kids Color
    & Draw by Bejoy Mobile, 94
  Kodable by SurfScore Inc., 85
  Magic Piano by Smule, 95
  MoMA Art Lab by the Museum
    of Modern Art, 94
  Scratch Jr. by Scratch Foundation, 85
Aprons, 73
Art center, 10
Art skills, 3, 41, 59, 88, 94–96
Assemblage artwork, 1–2
At-a-distance forces, 14–15
Audio recorders, 10, 43, 51
Axles, 20, 35–37

B

Balance, 33–34, 59, 62–64
Balloons, 46
Balls, 20, 22, 24, 26–28
Balsa wood, 64
Baskets, 24
Beans, 49
Block area, 10, 33, 61–63
Blocks, 27, 52, 64
Bolts, 22
Books, 11, 31
  Ada Lovelace, Poet of Science: The First
    Computer Programmer by Diane Stanley,
    87
  And Everyone Shouted Pull! A First Look at
    Forces and Motion by Claire Llewellyn, 37
  Boy + Bot by Ame Dyckman, 104
  Hello Ruby: Adventures in Coding by Linda
    Liukas, 86
  Hello Ruby: Journey Inside the Computer by
    Linda Liukas, 87
  How a House Is Built by Gail Gibbons, 74
  Iggy Peck, Architect by Andrea Beaty, 74
  The Listening Walk by Paul Showers, 57
  Mechanimals by Chris Tougas, 104
  Moonbear's Shadow by Frank Asch, 57
  The Most Magnificent Thing by Ashley
    Spires, 75
  Motion: Push and Pull, Fast and Slow by
    Darlene Stille, 37
  Robots, Robots, Everywhere! by Sue Fliess,
    104
  Rosie Revere, Engineer by Andrea Beaty, 37
  Sounds All Around by Wendy Pfeffer, 58
  The Three Little Pigs: An Architectural Tale by
    Steven Guarnaccia, 75
  Whose Shadow Is This? by Claire Berge, 57
Bowls, 73
Boxes, 20, 29, 49, 81
Brainstorming, 6
Bridges, 68–70
Bubble wrap, 28
Buckets, 66
Building, 59–75
  lesson ideas, 64–75
  with loose parts, 61–63

C

Calculators, 81
Card stock, 70
Cardboard tubes, 29, 46–47, 73
Cars, 20, 70
Cash registers, 81
Catapults, 24–26
Cause and effect, 76
Ceramic tiles, 64
Chairs, 31, 81
Chalk, 57
Clipboards, 33–35, 43, 50
Coding, 76–87
  lesson ideas, 80–86
Collaboration skills, 4, 6, 9, 11, 21–26, 28–33,
  36–37, 53–55, 64–74, 80–86, 88–104
  lesson ideas, 80–86, 94–104
Collaborative technology. See Interactive
  media
Colored cellophane, 54
Colors, 38, 52–55, 61, 64–66
Communication skills, 64–66, 68–70, 72–74,
  80–82, 84–86, 88–104
  lesson ideas, 80–86, 94–104
Comparing/contrasting, 52–53, 69

Computational thinkers, 78, 84–86
Computer programming. See Coding
Computers, 76–87, 79, 96
    dramatic play with, 80–82
Construction, 59–75
    lesson ideas, 64–75
Contact force, 15–16
Cooling racks, 50
Cooperation. See Collaboration skills
Cork, 64
Cotton balls, 24
Counting bears, 52
Craft sticks, 20, 22, 24, 64, 68, 73
Craft, Anna, 7–8
Crayons, 35
Creative communicators, 90–91
Creative thinking skills, 3, 5–7, 9, 59, 63,
    72–74
Critical thinking skills, 5–7, 59, 63, 78
Cups, 73

D
Data gathering, 17
Descriptive skills, 21–22, 26–28
Design challenges, 28–30
Design skills, 33–34, 59
Design-based learning, 1–3, 5
    promoting, 8–9
Digital cameras, 10–11, 29, 52, 67, 83, 96
Digital media, 10–11, 76–88, 98–104
Discovery learning, 5
Documentation skills, 7, 22–37, 43–45, 49–57,
    96–99, 102–104
Documenting children's work, 4, 9, 11
Dramatic play center, 10
    computers and, 80–82
Drums, 46–47
Duct tape, 73

E
Earth sciences, 10
Eggs, 29
Electrical force, 14–15
Electrical tape, 73
Empowered learners, 78, 84–86
Engineering design
    building/construction, 59–75
    force, 13, 16–17, 20–37
    light and shadow, 38–58
    motion, 6, 13–17, 20–37
    movement, 16, 18–19, 21–37, 78–79
    sound, 38–58, 94–96
Experimentation, 49–51
Exploration skills, 21–37, 43–57, 66–74,
    80–86, 94–104

F
Fabric, 29, 46, 64
Families. See Parent/community engagement
Flashlights, 53–55, 73

Force, 13, 15–17, 20
    identifying, 36
    lesson ideas, 21–37
Fred Rogers Center, 79–80, 88
Frequency, 38
Frictional force, 15
Frustration, 1–2, 18

G
Gears, 20
Gehry, Frank, 75
Global collaborators, 90–91
Globes, 81
Glue, 24, 29, 46, 73
Google Earth, 98–99
Google Maps, 98–99
Gravity
    defined, 14
    lesson ideas, 28–30
Gross motor skills, 13, 21–22
Guitars, 49

H
Hammers, 73
Headsets, 81
Hot-glue guns, 24, 46

I
Ice cube trays, 66
Idea experimentation, 6
"If-then-else" processing, 77–78
    lesson ideas, 82–84
Imagination, 8, 78
Immersion, 8
Inclined planes, 20, 36
Index cards, 33
Inertia, 16
Innovation, 8
Innovative designers, 78
Inquiry skills, 3, 6, 9
Interactive media, 89–90
International Society for Technology in
    Education, 7, 90–91
iPads, 10–11, 79, 85, 94, 98, 100

J
Johnson, Philip, 75
Journaling, 11, 22, 26–28, 53–55, 72–74

K
Kazoos, 47
Keyboards, 81, 96
Kitchen appliances, 96
Knowledge constructors, 78, 84–86

L
Language skills, 41, 76, 82–84, 88, 102–104
Learning centers, 10–12
Leaves, 61
Lego bricks, 20

Levers, 20, 36
Life sciences, 10, 91–93
Light and shadow, 38–58
   lesson ideas, 52–57
   understanding, 38
Light-tables, 52
Literacy skills, 3, 13, 76, 88

M
Magnetism, 14
Magnifying glasses, 73
Manmade materials, 1, 61
Maps, 98
Marbles, 27
Markers, 35, 46–47, 56
Masking tape, 21, 27, 47, 73
Mass, 16
Math skills, 3, 5, 13, 59, 76, 88
Matthews, Alice, 8
McConnon, Linda, 8
Measuring skills, 21–22, 26–28, 92
Measuring tapes, 73
Metal hooks, 50
Modeling clay, 64, 68
Molds, 66
Motion, 6, 13, 16–17, 20
   lesson ideas, 21–37
Movement, 78–79
   lesson ideas, 21–37
   straw gliders, 18–19, 33–34
Mud, 66
Muffin tins, 50
Music activities, 22, 46–49
Musical instruments, 46–49

N
National Academies Press, 7, 16–17, 39–40,
   60–61
National Association for the Education of
   Young Children, 7, 79, 88
Natural materials, 1, 61, 64
Negative space, 41
Newspaper, 29
Normal force, 15

O
Observation skills, 17, 21–22, 26–28, 36,
   64–66, 70–72, 91–93
Opaque objects, 39
   lesson ideas, 52–53, 55–57
Open-ended tasks, 5–6
Originality, 28–30
Outdoor spaces, 10, 24, 42, 45, 49–51, 55–57,
   63–64, 66–68

P
Paintbrushes, 73
Paints, 35, 46, 47
Pans, 50
Paper, 20, 22, 29, 33, 35, 50, 56, 68, 81, 96, 98

Parent/community engagement, 9, 11, 30,
   49–51, 74
Pencils, 22, 27, 29, 33, 35, 43, 47, 50, 70, 81,
   96, 98
   colored, 35, 54, 73
Pens, 20, 47, 81
Pictures, 64, 68, 81
Pipe cleaners, 22, 73
Pitch, 38, 44
Planning skills. See Strategic planning skills
Plastic animals, 56, 68
Plastic beads, 49
Plastic bottles, 49
Plastic planks, 27
Plastic trays, 22, 96
Plastic wrap, 54
Plates, 49
Play, 78–79
   defined, 8
   importance of, 4–5
Playdough, 68
Playground cones, 24
Pliers, 73, 96
Plywood, 64
Pompoms, 24
Possibility thinking, 7–9
Potato mashers, 50
Pots, 50
Predicting skills, 25, 27–30, 92
Print media, 11
Problem identification, 59–61, 68–70
Problem-solving skills, 3, 5–6, 9, 13, 17, 26–28,
   31–33, 46–53, 55–57, 64–68, 70–72, 76, 78,
   80–84, 94–96
Project-based learning, 1–3, 5
Projectors, 52
Properties of matter, 60
   lesson ideas, 64–72
Pulleys, 20, 31–33, 36

Q
Questioning skills, 5, 7–9, 17, 20, 42–43, 64,
   70–72, 80

R
Ramps, 26–28
Recycling/reusing, 1, 24–26, 28–30, 42, 49–51,
   72–74, 96–98
Reflection, 41
Reflective objects, 39
Remote controls, 96
Representation, 59
Revisiting ideas, 11, 52–53
Rice, 49
Risk taking, 4–6, 8
Rocks, 61
Ropes, 24, 31
Rubber bands, 20, 24, 29, 47, 54
Rulers, 47, 70, 73

S

Safety goggles, 73
Sand, 66
Sandpaper, 28
Scaffolding, 3, 5, 9, 39, 41, 82–84
Scales, 73
Scanners, 81
Science center, 55
Science skills, 3, 5, 13, 41, 59, 88
Scissors, 33, 46–47, 70, 73
Screwdrivers, 73, 96
Screws, 20, 22, 36, 50
Seashells, 61
Self-determination, 8
Self-regulatory skills, 61–63
Shakers, 49
Shapes, 6, 40, 61, 64–66
    strength of, 70–72
Sharing, 1, 9
Social studies, 3
Society for Technology in Education, 77–78
Solution finding skills, 22–30, 66–74, 84–86, 94–98
Sound, 38–58, 94–96
    lesson ideas, 43–51
    understanding, 38
Speed, 26–28
    lesson ideas, 22–24
Spoons, 50, 73
Spring force, 16
Stability, 59
Sticks, 61
Stones, 64
Storytelling, 102–104
Strategic planning skills, 9, 22–30, 46–51, 55–57, 59, 64–66, 76, 96–98
Straw flutes, 47
Straw gliders, 18–19, 33–34
Straws, 20, 22, 33, 47, 68, 73
String, 29, 49, 73
Structure, 6
Styrofoam trays, 22, 96

T

Tables, 81
Tablets, 10–11, 79, 85, 94, 98, 100
Taking turns, 25
Tambourines, 49
Tape measures, 27
Tape, 20, 22, 29, 33, 70
Teacher's role, 4–5, 9, 89–90
Technology/engineering
    communication/collaboration, 80–82, 88–104
    connecting to content areas, 9, 20
    knowledge/innovation, 76–87
    learning centers, 10–12, 20
    lesson ideas, 80–86, 94–104
Telephones, 81, 96

Tension force, 15
Testing designs, 17–18, 60–61, 68–70, 72–74
Three-dimensional structures, 1–2, 13, 59, 68–74
Tiles, 64
Timers, 73
Tinker Toys, 20
Tools, 3, 73, 96
Transformation, 6
Translucent objects, 39, 41
    lesson ideas, 52–55
Transparent objects, 39, 52
    lesson ideas, 52–55
Trials, 9, 26–28, 28–30
Twigs, 22
Twine, 73

U

Unit blocks, 63
Uprightness, 59

V

Velcro strips, 73
Velocity, 16
Vibration, 46–51
Visual complexity, 59
Visualization skills, 21–30, 43–55, 66–74, 80–82, 96–99
Volume, 38, 44

W

Wax paper, 28, 47
Websites
    Animoto, 102
    Annenburg Learner's Journey North, 91
    Boston Children's Museum, 100
    Code.org®, 77
    The Field Museum, 100
    foldnfly.com, 34
    Kizoa, 102
    Monterey Bay Aquarium, 100
    Museum of Modern Art, 100
    National Air and Space Museums, 102
    National Gallery of Art, 100
    Prezi, 102
    Smithsonian Museum of Natural History, 100
    Zoo Atlanta, 100
Wedges, 20, 36
Wheels, 20
    lesson ideas, 35–37
Wood screws, 50
Wood strips, 64, 73
Wooden logs, 31
Wooden planks, 27, 64
Wright, Frank Lloyd, 75

Z

Zip ties, 50